Seth Means War

The Blood-Stained Myth of the Egyptian God of Chaos

Christopher Fisher

Table of Contents

Introduction   6

Chapter 1: Egyptian Mythology for Beginners   9

The Start of Creation   9

The Concept of Ma'at   16

Death and the Afterlife   22

Humans in the Eyes of the Gods   23

Chapter 2: Egyptian Mythology's Place in Society   25

Egyptian Mythology in Ancient Egypt   26

Ancient Architecture   27

Science and Medicine   29

Societal Roles   30

Daily Practices   31

Film and Television   38

Books and Graphic Novels   40

Chapter 3: Godly Origins   42

Chapter 4: Varying Depictions of Seth   44

Iconography of Seth   46

The Use of Seth's Image in Ancient Egypt   49

Why Are Depictions of Seth So Inconsistent?   52

Chapter 5: Seth, Divine Protector or Evil Incarnate?   54

The World's First Murderer   58

Seth Versus Horus   61

The Duality of Seth and Horus   69

Chapter 6: Seth's Influence on Culture   71

Places of Worship												71
Seth's Contemporary Influence									75

Chapter 7: Man's Moral Struggles Mirror Seth's Legacy			78
Power Has Always Controlled Man								82
Literary Examples of Power and Corruption						92
Power Doesn't Have to Be a Bad Thing							97

Conclusion												99

About the Author											103

References												104

Image References											111

Introduction

Before humans had set their feet on the Earth, before there was even an Earth at all, the universe was nothing but vast darkness. Suddenly, out of the darkness, the gods emerged. First, there was one, the god of the sun. From him came two more, followed by another pair. Over time, thousands of gods and goddesses made up the ancient Egyptian pantheon, each with a unique origin and history. Some gods were rulers, keeping the peace on Earth while providing luscious lands on which humans would reside. Some gods were warriors, fighting monsters and creatures determined to destroy civilization. There were even gods who villainized the others, acting out of pure malevolence toward humanity and the structure of the universe.

And then, there were the gods who were so complex, so ambivalent, that their place in Egyptian mythology teeters between good and evil for eternity. The epitome of such a deity? Seth, the Egyptian god of war and chaos.

Throughout history, researchers have discovered countless depictions of Seth, ranging from hieroglyphic stories to imagery carved onto the walls of temples. With every discovery about the god of war, a new perspective is brought to the forefront of Egyptian mythology. Seth's infamy existed in nearly every part of ancient Egypt, even the deserted borders separating the country from foreign lands. These various depictions of Seth have proven to historians that the god is a complicated, largely misunderstood figure in ancient Egyptian mythology.

Seth Means War: The Blood-Stained Myth of the Egyptian God of Chaos will take you on a literary adventure to explore the complexities surrounding Seth's folklore. The following chapters hold within them the fascinating stories of protection, passion, and power. But before you can begin to understand the intricate details of Egyptian mythology, you must first understand the divine family tree. Beginning with the god Ra, this book will teach you the fundamental ideology behind each major god, including their origin stories and iconography.

Once you can confidently tell the difference between the gods and goddesses, you will learn about the ancient Egyptians' beliefs regarding life, death, and the afterlife. These topics were a huge component of everyday life during this time and the ancient civilization had specific beliefs about each phase of a soul's journey. *Seth Means War* will discuss the concept of Ma'at, ancient Egypt's moral code; how the underworld was depicted; and the individual pieces of a person that make up their soul.

From there, this book will delve into the long-lasting influence Egyptian mythology has had on ancient and modern societies. Architecture, science, and literature have been developed based on the lore told by the ancient people. Entire civilizations inspired by Egyptian mythology have emerged. Even today, the stories are reimagined as entertaining movies and novels in places like the USA and the United Kingdom. Seth and his divine family members are still being ingrained in history, just as they were 8,000 years ago. But why? This book will explore the many reasons behind societies' love of Egyptian mythology.

As for Seth's influence on society, you will learn about the many places of worship, kingdoms, and communities that were inspired by the god of chaos. From ancient Egyptian Dynasties to anti-establishment cults in 1970s America, Seth's reputation has become ingrained in human history. The god has been remembered as a villain, hero, and fool all at once, his identity dependent on the perspective of those who speak about him.

Most importantly, *Seth Means War* will make a staggering, but true, psychological connection between Seth and humankind. Unlike most gods and goddesses who are said to have unattainable abilities and potential, Seth represents the common struggles found on Earth. With moral uncertainty, an obsession with power, and complicated histories—humankind is more akin to the god of war and chaos than many people realize. Seth's moral ambivalence throughout ancient storytelling resembles the way human beings battle with choosing good over evil on a daily basis.

Power has the potential to change the world. In the right hands—that is, the hands of someone with good intentions—power may create greatness. However, there are people whose morals cannot withstand the desire to have control, much less the ability to obtain it. Having excess power over others has often destroyed societies, both in mythology and reality. Even a god as mighty as Seth could not overcome his desperation for power over the world.

The final chapter of this book will describe various historical events that exemplify the dangers of putting power in the wrong hands. These stories are widely-known across the world and have gone down in history as life-changing moments for humanity. Through analysis of the intentions behind each historical figure, you will learn just how common it is for someone to be overcome by their need for power, causing them to lose sight of their morality. Much like what you will learn in the myths about Seth, this insatiable desire for control can result in devastating consequences.

Chapter 1: Egyptian Mythology for Beginners

The Start of Creation

Unlike the religions of Christianity or Islam, which worship one almighty God, the beliefs of ancient Egypt were based on polytheism. Rather than living under the assumption that one deity is responsible for creating life, the ancient Egyptians believed in a large, extended family of gods and goddesses. Though this family, known as the Egyptian pantheon, stems from one original entity, each god and goddess serves a unique purpose and destiny. The pantheon is a complex, intertwining web of divine beings, most of which are still worshiped today, though in more modern ways. Throughout ancient history, over 2,000 Egyptian deities were worshiped and relied on by humankind. Each god and goddess represented an aspect of life, ranging from emotions and morals to elements and the cosmos.

According to Egyptian mythology, three things existed before the creation of life: darkness, the primeval ocean, and Atum, the creator god. In contrast to the gods you will learn about in this chapter, who existed in physical bodies and earthly representations, Atum existed as an intangible entity. He was an essence, if you will—a metaphysical consciousness.

When Atum felt the time was right to begin creation, he manifested himself in a more physical sense, creating from the vast ocean an island on which he could support himself. His physical form would forever be known as Ra, the sun god.

Ra

As the sun god, Ra harnesses the power of light. He brings warmth to the blossoming land before him. Due to his significant role in the creation of life and humanity, Ra's influence can be found in every part of Egyptian myth. He is often visually depicted as a falcon-headed man standing beneath the sun but has also been known to be represented as a scarab beetle. Though a simple beetle may initially seem unworthy of representing such an important figure, the scarab beetle held much significance to ancient Egyptians. It was believed that the insect was "self-created", like Ra himself (Haikal, 2022). That, along with the idea that scarab beetles emerge from the desert sand at the first sign of sunshine, established a strong connection between the small creature and the powerful deity.

From Ra came the first gods, Shu and Tefnut, who extended the divine family tree even further. The two children of Ra created Geb and Nut, from whom Osiris, Isis, Seth, and Nephthys were born. These are the primordial gods, the deities who gave rise to the intricate stories and myths that are still told to this day. Throughout history, these nine gods and goddesses have been referred to as the Ennead of Heliopolis, the city of the Sun God.

Shu

Shu was the first son of Ra. His name means *dry*, which perfectly suits his responsibility as the god of air and dryness. Combined with the heat from his father's mighty sun, Shu represents the warm air that cascades over the Egyptian sands. His calm, flowing presence as a deity eventually established him as a god of peace, in addition to air and dryness. Shu is often depicted as a human man with a headdress of feathers, though the size and significance of the feathers varies throughout ancient imagery.

Tefnut

The goddess of moisture, including dew and rain, is Shu's counterpart and consort. Her name is Tefnut, the daughter of Ra. In most ancient Egyptian imagery, Tefnut can be seen as a human woman with the head of a lioness, often standing with a sun disk placed upon her head. Many variations of the mythology surrounding Tefnut declare that she was "spat into existence" by her father, Ra (National Geographic, 2017). She and her brother Shu are known as the first couple of the Ennead, joining forces as husband and wife to create more gods and goddesses of great power.

It is important to note that, in the complicated case of Egyptian mythology, gods being both siblings and spouses was not uncommon. On the contrary, many of the deities you will learn about are closely related in more than one way. This connection was not viewed as abnormal or taboo in the eyes of ancient Egyptians, nor by those who study Egyptian mythology today. Because the gods and goddesses were the first of their kind to exist, they did not abide by the same beliefs on familial reproduction as most modern human beings do.

Geb

Once created, the god of air and the goddess of moisture joined forces to give birth to two divine offspring. Their son, Geb, was born as the god of the Earth. As the Earth god, Geb had immense power over earthly phenomena, such as earthquakes and the growth of plants and vegetation. Naturally, this power resulted in Geb's high regard for humans, as he allowed them to live and prosper on his land.

In hieroglyphic imagery, Geb is represented by the symbol of a goose. However, it is also common to see the god depicted as a snake. Personified, Geb can be found in the form of a human man with a goose atop his head, or as a man with the head of a goose or snake. He is often shown in images alongside his twin sister, the goddess Nut, as well. The two share a deep bond, one that comes with its own fascinating mythology. It is believed that, upon their creation, Geb and his sister emerged holding one another tightly in their arms.

Nut

Geb's twin sister and consort, Nut, is known as the goddess of the sky. When she and her brother were born, intertwined in each other's arms, their father chose to pull them apart. Their separation by the god of air is representative of the physical distance between the sky and the earth, with air lingering in between. Nut is also said to protect her grandfather, Ra, by holding him in her stomach at nighttime and giving birth to him in the morning, symbolizing the rise and fall of the sun.

Nut, pronounced like *newt*, is depicted rather uniquely in ancient Egyptian imagery. In addition to being represented as a large cow, the goddess is often shown balancing on her fingertips and toes, arched over her brother, Geb. In some depictions, Nut's body is covered in stars, showing her as the night sky. There were ancient Egyptians that even believed that the placement of her fingers and toes coincided with the north, south, east, and west points.

With the help of her brother-husband, Nut gave birth to four children: Osiris, Isis, Nephthys, and Seth. Variations of this myth sometimes suggest that there were five children of Nut, with the inclusion of Horus the Elder. However, Horus is more often believed to be the son of Isis and Osiris.

Osiris

Osiris is the firstborn son of Nut and Geb and the consort of the goddess Isis. Though he is the god of many aspects of the universe, Osiris is most famously referred to as the Lord of the Earth. Being the son of the earth god, Osiris reigns over fertility and agriculture, praised by humankind for his kind nature, gift of abundance, and generosity. He taught human beings how to cultivate their lands and make the most out of the plants that sprung from the earth.

Osiris was killed by his younger brother, Seth, who was driven into action by his feelings of resentment and jealousy. Despite his gruesome murder, the ruling god was revived by his sister-wife, Isis, and became "Lord and Judge of the Dead" (Mark, 2016a). His resurrection inspired humankind to regard him as a symbol of new life and hope for rebirth. According to myths and ancient imagery, Osiris was seen in various forms. One personification of the god showed him as a king, wearing a crown and carrying royal belongings. He is also depicted as a mummified version of his human form in many paintings and drawings from ancient times. Frequently, Osiris is shown with dark green or black skin, symbolizing the rejuvenating mud from the Nile River.

Isis

Isis is the sister-wife of Osiris, responsible for bringing him back to life and bearing his son, Horus. Though she is considered the goddess of magical healing and motherhood, Isis has multiple roles in ancient Egyptian mythology. Being the representative goddess for mothers and fertility, she was highly regarded as the gold standard for women. Humankind looked up to her and prayed for her healing powers, building temples and performing rituals in her honor. Isis was and still is worshiped all over Egypt. Thanks to her deep connection to Osiris and his rebirth, she is also seen as a protector of kings and pharaohs.

Isis is symbolized in many different ways, some of which include a falcon and an empty throne. In human form, Isis is often depicted as a beautiful woman in a queen's dress. Some images of the personified goddess show her with horns on her head, and the sun disk resting in between. Other images replace the horns and sun disk with the symbol for the empty throne. Throughout her mythology, Isis is also represented by the image of a bird, scorpion, or cow.

After resurrecting her true love, Isis was so filled with joy that she used her magic to impregnate herself with Osiris' child. Their child, Horus, would eventually become one of the most powerful and well-known deities in ancient Egyptian mythology.

Nephthys

Nephthys, the second daughter of Nut and Geb, is the goddess of darkness, mourning, and protection of the dead. Similarly to her sister, Nephthys was also believed to possess magical powers and healing abilities. The goddess was often involved in funerary services and was frequently called upon for protection during the night. Her image is akin to that of Isis and, according to some myths, the two were considered identical in almost every way. The main difference between the two goddesses is their headdresses. While Isis is portrayed with a throne or bull's horns on her head, Nephthys is most often shown with the hieroglyphic symbol for *house* as a headdress.

Most resources claim that Nephthys played few roles in Egyptian myths besides helping her sister revive Osiris. Despite her powers and significance during death, she is primarily known for being the sister-wife of the god Seth and one of many catalysts for the conflict between Seth and Osiris.

Seth

Seth, the fourth child of Nut and Geb, and the subject of this book, is a complicated fixture in ancient Egyptian mythology. There are countless stories and myths in which Seth is described as a villain, a force of evil in comparison to his divine family. Yet, Seth's history is not exclusively filled with tales of destruction and chaos. His purpose as a member of the Ennead was more than what is frequently told. Originally, Seth used his great might to protect the other gods from enemies. He was granted the responsibility to help the dead travel to the afterlife. In many ways, Seth began his journey as a hero.

But, like many heroes, all it took was a small taste of power to turn Seth's greatness into destruction.

The Concept of *Ma'at*

The ancient Egyptians had strong moral integrity. Humans and gods alike believed in living honorably with justice and truth at the forefront of every thought and action. It was widely acknowledged that adhering to these morals would bring balance to the universe, a type of harmony that pleased the gods and maintained order in the universe. This is the concept of Ma'at.

As well as being a concept, Ma'at is personified as a goddess with the same name. She reigns over law, order, justice, truth, and harmony—everything that makes up the ideology through which she was created. The goddess Ma'at was honored in every ancient Egyptian city, her ideals known by all who existed at the time. Today, the concept of Ma'at is seen as a philosophy. In ancient times, it was a way of life that, if followed, would eventually lead to an eternal paradise. In order to reach such an afterlife, however, ancient Egyptians would undergo an important test after they met their death. In the Duat, the Egyptian underworld, souls of the deceased traveled to the Hall of Judgment. It was in this place that a person would officially find out if they were going to reach a blissful afterlife or spend eternity in the darkness of the Duat.

The process, while frightening for the souls being judged, is truly fascinating. In the Hall of Judgment, a person's heart would be weighed on a scale against the Feather of Ma'at. The feather represents the ideals of the goddess Ma'at. If the scales were tipped in favor of the feather, the person's heart was viewed as good, having followed the goddess' moral standards during life. For those whose hearts outweighed the Feather of Ma'at, an endless future in the underworld awaited. To make the matter more gruesome, the heavy hearts would be consumed by the goddess Ammit, a name that roughly translates to "devourer of the dead." With their hearts taken by Ammit, the souls of the deceased would cease to exist entirely, leaving them lifeless and without purpose in the Duat. It was a fate worse than anything else in the eyes of ancient Egyptian citizens.

Before a person received their judgment, while their heart rested on the scale, they would confess to the 42 ideals of Ma'at. Such confessions began with a salutation to their respective god, followed by the moral actions taken by the person during their time on Earth. The 42 confessions included stating that one has not stolen from the gods, lived with unprovoked anger, or performed any evil (Kemet Experience, 2019). Whether or not these confessions were true was to be decided by the scale.

Death and the Afterlife

The concept and process of death in ancient Egypt are known by many, even those who do not associate themselves with the ancient religion or mythology. Thanks to modern media and historical museums, the world has been made aware of ancient Egyptians' unique perspectives on dying. Mummified bodies, sarcophagi, and sacred tombs have been identified and explored by people on almost every continent. The people of ancient Egypt were devoted to their rituals, ensuring a soul's safe passage to the afterlife.

To mummify a deceased body simply means to embalm, or preserve, it. It was a task that took several weeks to accomplish, beginning with removing the organs and internal body parts. Preventing the body from internal decay was a major component of preserving the entire body. Religious figures would perform rituals and other duties while embalming the bodies, reciting prayers for the soul that would soon be transitioning. Most of the time, due to the expensive nature of the process, only highly regarded people would be mummified and built a tomb for eternal rest. These people included pharaohs, nobility, and the wealthiest citizens.

Once the organs were removed, the body would be dried out and wrapped in linens. In the same way that Western societies restore bodies before placing them in a casket, ancient Egyptians took the time to raise any sunken areas of the skin and add false eyes to create a more recognizable human face. In their tombs, mummified bodies would be surrounded by the possessions they used when living, like artwork and furniture. The religion of ancient Egypt followed the belief that these items would be carried through the afterlife to provide daily comforts to their owner.

The Soul

The ancient Egyptians believed a person's soul was made up of nine individual components. Though separate, each part of the soul was connected. If one aspect was missing or lacking, the rest of the soul would not be complete.

First, there is the *Khat*. This is the physical body that houses one's soul during life. The Khat is the vessel through which a soul can live as a human being, taking in the Earth's nutrients and wonders, provided by the gods. The physical body also allowed ancient Egyptians to worship their gods and goddesses, reciting prayers in their honor and creating beautiful tributes.

Alongside the physical body are a person's spiritual body and power, the *Sah* and *Sechem*. The spiritual body, Sah, was achieved when a person's physical body was properly preserved, and they were judged well against the Feather of Ma'at. The Sah gave a person's soul the ability to exist in the afterlife and communicate with the entities that existed in that realm. The Sechem represents the power of one's soul to transform. In a way, it is considered the life force or power behind a person's spiritual body.

Similarly to the Sah, the *Ka* was a person's "double-form" (Mark, 2019). It is said that, while a person is alive in human form, their Ka is within them, benefiting from the nourishment of food and water. When that person's body dies, the Ka is released, only being brought back to the body when it has been preserved. The Ka is the essence of life within each soul.

The *Ab*, or heart, of a person is an integral part of their soul, as it is the part of a person that is weighed in the Hall of Judgment. The Ab is the source of a person's morality, or lack thereof. It contains both good and evil, though the balance between them is different for every person.

A person's individuality and personality are contained within their soul's *Ba*, which is sometimes depicted as a bird flying out of the tomb that houses the physical body. The Ba brings a person's unique traits on their travel to the afterlife, maintaining their personal experience as a living being. It is what differentiates all of the souls from one another.

The final two components of a person's soul are their *Shuyet*, or shadow self, and their *Ren*, meaning their name and identity. The shadow self exists in tandem with the physical body and is often said to be the version of a person that is left after their body has died. Though they are not a complete person after death, they still exist in their shadow. A person's name, Ren, provides an intimate connection with their identity. Most ancient Egyptians were given names that held significant meaning to Egyptian life or religion. It is also believed that, without a name, a person would be unable to prosper in the afterlife.

At last, when a person has transformed from physical existence to spiritual, they are one with their *Akh*. The Akh is the enlightened, immortal version of the person that once existed. It is the combination of the many virtues, choices, and transformations that a soul goes through during life and death. Together with the other components of the soul, the Akh gives a deceased person the ability to reach the Hall of Judgment.

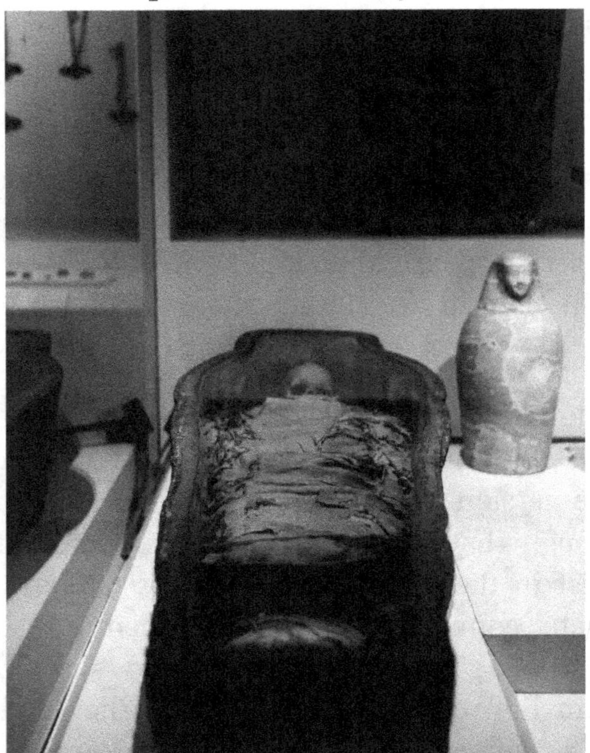

The Field of Reeds

As previously mentioned, the everyday choices of ancient Egyptians were greatly influenced by the idea of an afterlife. For most citizens, there was no possibility that dying meant an immediate halt in one's existence. Instead, a deceased person gets one of two opportunities: to live forever in the dark, empty Duat or to find eternal peace and bliss. To achieve the latter, one's soul must be proven pure when weighed against the Feather of Ma'at before they are granted entrance into the Field of Reeds.

Those who made it to the Field of Reeds were known as the justified dead, the souls that had been proven worthy on the scale of Ma'at. Once they were justified, they had the ability to communicate with the gods and goddesses in ways they were never able to while living on Earth. On some occasions, the justified dead were sought out by the deities to help fight enemies and maintain order in the universe.

The Field of Reeds is similar to the idea of Heaven, paradise, or Valhalla in other religions. It is a place in one's afterlife that is filled with joy and purity.

Humans in the Eyes of the Gods

The Egyptian myth of humanity's creation is, simply put, a story of a father's love for his children. After creating his son and daughter, Shu and Tefnut, Ra sent them off into the new world to continue his creation. When Seh and Tefnut were gone, Ra felt an emptiness that could only be described as a deep longing for his only children. He removed his eye and gave it the ability to seek out his son and daughter, quite literally keeping his eye on them.

Ra waited, alone, on the primordial hill. Eventually, Shu and Tefnut returned to him, followed by the Eye of Ra. The family reunion is believed to have been incredibly emotional for the god Ra. According to the myth, he was so happy to have his children safely returned that he began to shed tears. Human beings materialized as each tear reached the fertile hill beneath the gods. Men and women, completely new to the world and lacking the necessities for survival, looked toward the gods for guidance. Shu and Tefnut created their own children, Gen and Nut, to provide a home for their grandfather's creations. From then on, the gods cared for the humans and gave them the many things needed to carry on a life of their own. In return, the humans abided by the gods' and goddesses' rules and desires.

Each god viewed humankind from a different perspective, though many regarded human life as something to be influenced and manipulated, whether with good intentions or bad. Some gods and goddesses, like Osiris and Isis, chose to educate human beings and teach them how to live successfully on Earth. The humans were given gifts of nature and knowledge, as well as protection by their benevolent deities. In the case of the goddess Ma'at, human beings were allowed opportunities to grow into virtuous people, abiding by the laws of harmony and peace. However, some gods took advantage of humankind and wanted to rule over them with malice, controlling their every move.

No matter what the perspective on human beings, each god and goddess was fueled by the love bestowed onto them by their creations. In order to receive the benefits from a god, like cures for illnesses or fertile lands, humans were required to pay their utmost respect to the god that provided what they needed. By calling out their names in prayer and performing rituals for the gods, humans were rewarded. Temples and cults were established for many of the gods and goddesses, providing the deities with the attention and worship they desired.

For the humans that lived in line with the gods' morals and virtues, an eternal lifetime beside the divine creatures was awarded. This was the ultimate goal in the eyes of ancient Egyptians.

Chapter 2: Egyptian Mythology's Place in Society

As time has progressed, Egyptian mythology's influence on society has evolved. In the ancient years, hearing stories about divine beings and dedicating one's life to them was commonplace. Although there were, of course, some people who refused to live by the gods' laws, most citizens in ancient Egypt believed in mythology as a religion. Over centuries, those beliefs became less and less popular, due in part to the influx of other religions and dominating kingdoms.

Despite this rise in new beliefs, Egypt's unique religious system persevered through the architecture, tales, and practices of the Egyptian people. In time, Egypt became a more modern country, as is the case for most, but its people have always been connected to their ancient roots.

Even Western societies, like Europe and the Americas, have been influenced by Egyptian mythology for millennia. Egyptian civilization is said to have formed before ancient Greece, but just by a few decades. Many of the gods in Greek mythology resemble or are exactly like the Egyptian gods, as well. The myths themselves are different, as is the origin of humankind—however, there are significant similarities between the roles of deities in both ancient Egypt and ancient Greece.

Through a more modern lens, Egyptian mythology plays a large role in Westernized media and entertainment. The myths have been included in curricula at universities, ranging from classes about ancient languages to archaeology. There are countless works of literature written about or based on ancient Egyptian religion, including children's books and plays. What's more, numerous movies and television shows have been produced that reimagine the myths and ideas.

The influence of ancient Egypt reaches the farthest corners of the world, keeping the enchanting beliefs and stories alive for the people of today.

Egyptian Mythology in Ancient Egypt

Egyptian civilization began so long ago that historians and archaeologists cannot be sure of the exact starting point. Most academics and researchers agree that ancient Egypt started around 6000 B.C.E, over 8,000 years ago. The mythology came soon after. Nearly every aspect of ancient life was influenced by Egyptian religion. Temples and pyramids were built and art was created to honor the gods and goddesses. Religion even impacted social structure: The ancient Egyptians believed the gods designed society as a mirror image of themselves. Therefore, people were not encouraged to disrupt the societal classes. Kings were chosen by the gods and goddesses for specific reasons, as were the people at the lowest end of the social system.

Without ancient Egyptian religion, much of the architecture of the time would have looked entirely different. Because of the beliefs surrounding death and the afterlife, certain buildings and structures were formed to house the dead. Tombs were built for those in the ancient civilization who were highly regarded, like kings and nobility. These unique burial chambers gave the deceased members of society a place of comfort as they transitioned to the afterlife.

In a similar sense, the pyramids in Egypt were built for housing the tombs. Throughout many decades of research and archaeological study, Egyptologists have been able to explore the burial chambers created thousands of years ago, identifying preserved bodies of kings and their belongings. There is quite a lot of speculation about how the ancient Egyptians built the pyramids, especially without modern technology or machinery.

The Great Sphinx of Giza is another historical landmark in Egypt, one that has stood the test of time. Created in the image of the Sphinx, a mythological creature that became a symbol in ancient Egypt, the giant statue towers over the sand. Ancient Egyptians carved the statue out of limestone, forming it into the body of a lion with a human head wearing a headdress. It measures about "240 feet long and 66 feet high" (Tikkanen, 2017).

Large buildings were also built as a place in which citizens could honor their gods and goddesses. These buildings, called temples, were crucial components of living in ancient Egypt. Temples provided a space where people could show their respect for the deities through prayer, rituals, and protection of their god's statue inside the temple. Other activities occurred within the holy buildings, as well, like weddings and funerals. Temples were also beautifully ornate and decorated with ancient drawings and hieroglyphs. The walls of most temples were filled with symbols of the gods and goddesses for which the temples were built, reminding each person who enters the building that their gods were with them. Carvings of godly creatures and divine beings were made on the columns inside the temple, some as tall as the ceiling above.

Temples were located all over ancient Egypt, each one built specifically for the god that reigned over the surrounding area. Even today, over 8,000 years later, the intricate artwork and architecture of Egyptian temples can be observed, unmoved from their place of origin. Archaeologists and historians work tirelessly to maintain the beauty of these buildings so that they can survive even more millennia.

Science and Medicine

The people of ancient Egypt did not ignore the importance of health and wellness. Researchers have found that the treatment of illnesses and injuries involved a combination of supernatural and natural remedies, including prayer, herbal medicine, and surgery. In fact, it is believed that the ancient Egyptians were the first to have professional doctors, a "respected occupation" (Brazier, 2018). The medical knowledge passed down by this ancient civilization is still used today in many cultures.

Gods and goddesses were at the forefront of medical practices. For someone who suffered from mental illnesses, it was believed that they were being overtaken by an evil spirit or punished by an angry god. The ancient people also believed that the power of magical healing was partially responsible for a person's cured ailment. Multiple deities, like Isis and another goddess named Heka, were known for their affinity to heal others. Carvings and images of Isis' presence during a child's birth have been discovered, a reminder of her healing power and protection of mothers. In addition to the magic of the gods, ancient Egyptian healers also relied on objects like amulets and statues to promote healing.

Societal Roles

Under the watchful eye of the goddess Ma'at, who reigned over harmony and justice, most ancient Egyptians lived their lives with gratitude and good intentions. They knew that if they caused chaos among themselves, it would disrupt the harmony established by the gods and result in severe posthumous consequences. Those who lived in the lowest societal classes typically did not fight to be part of a higher class because they believed they were placed exactly where the gods and goddesses wanted them. As with many cultures and societies, there were underprivileged people, even those who were hired as slaves. However, some research suggests that every person in ancient Egyptian civilization did their best to make the most out of life. This meant being good-hearted and pursuing acts of purity and morality.

Though there was little room for moving through social classes, as everyone had their own divinely-chosen place in society, some lower-class people were given special opportunities. Those who were skilled in the arts and other laborious tasks were sometimes reimbursed for their work in greater ways than those who were without certain skills. That is, the people who could help with the sculpting of statues and other holy artworks would be regarded more highly than others who only contributed to physical labor. This was often the case during the process of building pyramids and major landmarks.

Daily Practices

The daily lives of ancient Egyptian citizens consisted of many activities that are experienced in the 21st century. Although there were no cell phones or the Internet, the ancient people had various ways of staying entertained. Sports, games, contests, and festivals were popular among every social class, depending on accessibility.

Recreational Activities

The ancient Egyptians worked hard, but they played even harder. Pastimes like archery, swimming, and dancing filled the free time of most people, especially children. A board game called Senet was particularly popular, as it has been found in many tombs of ancient Egyptians. The game was similar to the game of checkers, in which two players played against each other and attempted to be the last player with playable pawns on the gameboard. Some ancient artwork also depicts the gods playing Senet, according to the World History Encyclopedia (Mark, 2017b). People also performed reenactments of the myths they believed in, such as the interactions between the gods Seth and Horus, which provided many entertaining stories.

Festivals and Events

There were many festivals and events held in honor of the Egyptian gods and goddesses, some of which included celebrations of the deities' birthdays and anniversaries of their great contributions to humanity. Some festivals were celebrated through feasts, while others involved musical performances and floral decorations, depending on the god being honored. Funerals, births, and housewarming events each had their own specific requirements, such as style of clothing and behaviors conducted. Funerals were events that required respectful clothing and behavior, while other celebrations allowed people to dress as they wanted and indulge in behaviors like drinking alcohol and dancing.

Law and Order

The ancient Egyptians had certain ways to deal with people who committed crimes or acts that went against the rules of the gods. Just like in the afterlife, Egyptian civilizations built buildings in which criminals would be judged. These buildings were called Judgment Halls and were reflections of the Hall of Judgment one would attend after physical death.

Judgment Halls could be buildings built in major cities, in which hearings and verdicts would be assigned. Lawful judgments could also be held in the marketplaces of smaller towns, where townspeople could observe. All judgments made by officials were made with respect to the goddess Ma'at, ensuring the same principles and morals were followed through life and the afterlife. The earlier years of ancient Egypt involved heavy emphasis on a local court to determine if a person was guilty or innocent of a crime. The local court consisted of "community leaders of sound moral judgment", who were relied upon to judge following the gods' perspectives (Mark, 2016d).

Punishments for crimes varied, depending on the severity of the circumstances. For most minor cases, a monetary fine was given to the culprit. If the crime was worse than something as minor as, say, petty theft, the punishment could be much more violent. In situations where the criminal has committed an assault of any kind or murder, the punishment could be as severe as the death penalty. Sometimes, a criminal could be lucky enough to avoid punishment by death and simply be physically mutilated, in the form of amputation of a body part. Needless to say, if such a significant crime was committed while a person was living, they would most likely face the ultimate punishment of being sentenced to eternity in the Duat, rather than the Field of Reeds.

Egyptian Mythology in Modern-Day Egypt

Much of ancient Egyptian culture has been pushed aside to make room for newer, more modern takes on daily life. No matter how modern the times get, however, Egypt will always be a country that holds immense historical and mythological significance.

In addition to the many university courses and majors that are based on Egyptology, the study of Egypt, there are various businesses and tourist attractions that focus on ancient Egyptian landmarks. Today, almost anyone can book a tour to visit the pyramids or the Great Sphinx and revel in the historical greatness.

The Pyramids of Giza are certainly the most sought-after tourist attraction in Egypt. Considered the only surviving location of the Seven Wonders of the world, the pyramids have captured the attention of researchers for centuries. No one is absolutely sure about how the pyramids were built and the mystery is a major controversy for many. It's typically suggested that thousands of human men worked for weeks to build the pyramids, but some people believe the ancient Egyptians had help from divine beings or unknown technology.

Tourists and researchers today can explore other places in Egypt that were inspired by mythology, as well. Temples all over the country are open for people to visit, as long as they respect the sanctity of the building. There are monasteries, too, that many tourists enjoy exploring. Interestingly enough, there are even boat cruises that take tourists on a scenic trip down the Nile, the river that was once revered by the ancient people for its powers of fertility and significance to the god Osiris.

Unfortunately for the ancient gods and goddesses, the reach of mythology in the modern world extends to tourist attractions and archaeological sites. For the most part, modern-day Egyptians do not have an organized following of the ancient religion, as other cultures have emerged in the country. Christianity and Islam are some of the most popular organized religions in Egypt right now, leaving little room for the religious influence of the Egyptian deities. However, in lesser-known pockets of the country, there are still people who show respect to the ancient gods by performing certain rituals and giving acknowledgment to the fascinating mythology.

Egyptian Mythology in Western Societies

Because ancient Egypt was one of the first civilizations to exist, it served as an inspiration for many of the civilizations that followed its establishment. The ancient Greeks translated and reimagined the various myths and stories during the Hellenistic period, allowing Western civilizations to understand them in written form. It wasn't until the early 19th century that Western researchers were able to decipher ancient Egyptian texts, so they relied heavily on the interpretations made by the ancient Greeks.

The mythology of ancient Egypt was recorded by philosophers and religious figures at the time, which influenced the development of Western ideas on religion, ideology, and mythology. Ancient Greek historians like Herodotus recorded the many mythological creatures and stories that he learned about on his visits to ancient Egypt, taking the information back home with him to ancient Greece.

University Programs

In more modern years, colleges and universities have embraced the alluring history of ancient Egypt, creating courses of study that center around the myths and lore of the civilization. Students who showed interest in the mythology of ancient Egypt could broaden their understanding of the subject by taking classes in Egyptology, Mythology, and even Classical Languages. To this day, universities like Brown and Cornell offer courses that educate learners about the ancient religion. The former even has an entire department dedicated to Egyptology.

Written Language

Written language is quite possibly the most influential aspect of ancient Egypt. Hieroglyphs, as you have learned, are commonly used to depict the gods and goddesses in writings about the myths. This style of writing is *pictorial*, meaning the words and phrases were written as illustrations, rather than letters. One may assume that each hieroglyph is associated with whatever the illustration resembles, however, this is not exactly the case. Each hieroglyph is different. Some represent the actual subjects of the illustration, such as the hieroglyphs for the gods and goddesses. Others represent individual sounds that coincide with spoken words. There are even hieroglyphs that indicate certain ideas and concepts (Kiger, 2021). It is a complex system of writing that has perplexed researchers and philosophers for millennia.

While the hieroglyphic language is a popular area of study among researchers, it is far from the only form of written language used by the ancient Egyptians. Hieratic and demotic writing were also common at the time. The former is a style of cursive writing that was frequently used in ancient papyri. According to linguists and Egyptologists, hieratic writing was a more convenient and casual style for the ancient people. It was developed as an alternate way of writing due to how complicated hieroglyphs were to write and understand.

Demotic writing is another style that was developed as an alternative to hieroglyphs. Like hieratic writing, from which this style is derived, demotic writing is a cursive script. It was most commonly used in "everyday documents and literary works," as well as in funerary literature (Selden, 2013). Researchers of ancient Egyptian languages have described it as a more abbreviated, or shortened, version of hieratic writing.

In 1799, a major discovery was made that would change the world's perception of written language. French soldiers invaded Egypt, led by dictator Napoleon Bonaparte, and ravaged the country with the intention of placing it under France's control. The soldiers found various treasures and foreign documents during their seizure of the country, including a stone slab covered in carved writing. The slab, known today as the Rosetta Stone, featured three different written languages: hieroglyphic writing, demotic writing, and ancient Greek. Presumably, the stone was created by the ancient Greek philosophers who wanted to translate the writings of ancient Egypt into their own language.

15 years after the French troops discovered the Rosetta Stone, a British scientist started studying the languages. The scientist was able to figure out that some of the hieroglyphs represented royal figures, the symbols indicating specific ways of pronouncing the names of ancient pharaohs (Kiger, 2021). A few years later, a linguist from France got access to the stone slab. Using the knowledge gained by the previous scientist to study the writing, the linguist determined the meaning behind the ancient text. According to his findings, the Rosetta Stone was a message sent from ancient Egyptian priests to the pharaoh Ptolemy V, written in 196 B.C.E (Kiger, 2021).

The discovery of the Rosetta Stone, along with the knowledge it brought to Western societies, changed how humanity perceived ancient texts. It provided new insight into what life was like in ancient Egypt, in addition to giving future linguists and writers a means of deciphering texts from thousands of years ago. Not only that, but it is the namesake of an incredibly popular language-learning software company that has allowed people to learn new languages with ease. Without the discovery and study of the Rosetta Stone, we may have never learned many of the Egyptian myths that inspired this book.

Egyptian Mythology in 20th- and 21st-Century Pop Culture

In addition to the classical and academic interpretations of Egyptian mythology, Western societies frequently indulge in making ancient stories their own. Numerous movies and television shows reimagine the myths to entertain the masses, many of which have seen massive success. Contemporary authors have also taken a keen interest in creating novels inspired by and including the Egyptian deities.

Film and Television

The 1999 film *The Mummy* was considered a box-office success, amassing over $400 million dollars upon its theatrical release. The film, which was followed by three sequels, is about a team of archaeologists who accidentally awaken a mummified priest from ancient Egypt. To make matters worse, the "mummy" was cursed as punishment for a crime before his death, causing him to wreak havoc against the archaeologists who are trying to help him find his place in the afterlife. With a cast led by actor Brendan Fraser, the movie was and still is a widely-known piece of Western entertainment.

Another film inspired by Egyptian mythology is *Gods of Egypt*, released in 2016. Although it is not as well-loved as *The Mummy*, it features famous actors like Gerard Butler, Nikolaj Coster-Waldau, and the late Chadwick Boseman. *Gods of Egypt* follows the myth of the gods Seth and Horus and their battle for the throne. The film includes a number of other gods, as well, including Isis, Osiris, and Nephthys. In many ways, the filmmakers took creative liberties with the mythology, reimagining it as a story about a human man who works alongside Horus to defeat Seth. On top of that, all of the gods are represented as human beings, without the specific headdresses or crowns that signify who is who. It's safe to say the film is an entertaining creation, but not entirely accurate to Egyptian mythology.

In 2022, a television series featuring a plethora of Egyptian myths and characters was added to the Marvel franchise. The series, *Moon Knight*, is both a story of a superhero and a reimagined take on Egyptian gods and the afterlife. In *Moon Knight*, the main characters meet various gods on their journey to defeat the antagonist, a man who worshiped the heart-devouring goddess Ammit. The main characters are given the gifts of Khonshu, the Egyptian moon god. Khonshu leads the characters on their journey, rather forcefully, to stop the worldwide damage the antagonist and Ammit are causing.

The entire series includes imagery and symbols of ancient Egypt, particularly those associated with the gods and goddesses. Using computer-generated imagery, the deities are shown in more mythologically accurate forms. Ammit, for example, resembles the ancient drawings of her complex form: a crocodile's head with the front legs of a lion and the hind legs of a hippopotamus. It is clear that the creators of the series took the time to reimagine the peculiar myths in a way that would be as accurate as possible while maintaining the show's fictional-fantasy theme. Toward the end of the series, the main characters even travel to the Duat and are brought to the Hall of Judgment, where their hearts are weighed against the Feather of Ma'at. Viewers are currently eagerly awaiting the release of a new season for the series.

Egyptian mythology has even made appearances in popular music videos. The video for Michael Jackson's song "Remember the Time" features ancient Egyptian imagery. Katy Perry has also included similar imagery and symbolism in her music video for the song "Dark Horse."

Books and Graphic Novels

Rick Riordan is a young adult author known for his intriguing perspectives on mythology. In addition to a series of books about Greek mythology, Riordan has published a trilogy inspired by ancient Egyptian religion. Similarly to the movies and films previously mentioned, the books are written with a fictional flair and include characters that were never a part of the original Egyptian myths. Nevertheless, the *Kane Chronicles* book series is a huge hit with fans of Riordan's novels, as well as adolescents interested in connecting with ancient Egypt.

A quick search on Goodreads.com for Egyptian-inspired novels reveals over 400 matches. Books about romances, adventures, and fantasy battles set in Egyptian mythology are very popular with readers today. There are also a large number of educational works about the unique facts and myths of ancient times.

Egyptian myths have also inspired graphic novels series. For instance, the *Moon Knight* television series is based on a graphic novel of the same name. The comic was first published in the 1980s, over 40 years ago. Issues of the series were released over four years, detailing the adventures and combats involving the Egyptian gods and the humans they control.

The colorful, fantastical scenes depicted in Egyptian mythology have undoubtedly inspired artists, creators, and storytellers for centuries. Even today, stories are being told in new ways, further immortalizing the ancient religion.

Chapter 3: Godly Origins

In his article featured in the *Journal of the American Research Center in Egypt*, Eugene Cruz-Uribe describes any attempt at understanding the complexities of Seth as an "elusive venture" (Cruz-Uribe, 2009). The role Seth plays throughout mythology evolves drastically, alongside contradictory perspectives and biases. In ancient Egypt, Seth was infamous. His violent crimes and domineering personality were some of the first things brought to mind at the mention of his name. There were, however, some ancient folk who worshiped the god.

Yet, Seth was not always well-known for his wrongdoings. In the earliest years of existence, the god of war and chaos was similar to his divine family members.

Seth's Beginnings

Though he evolved from a mostly-benevolent god to one who craved destruction, Seth's affinity for violence stuck with him from the beginning. A description of Seth's birth is included in the Pyramid Texts, a work of literature from the Egyptians that is said to be the oldest funerary text from ancient Egypt. In the text, Seth's birth is described as violent. The text states that Seth "broke through his mother's side and leaped forth," foreshadowing his eternity as a violently exciting god (Turner, 2012). Some researchers suggest that, due to his unnatural birth, Seth was associated with miscarriages and childbirth issues (Rikala, 2007). Like his siblings, Seth was born from the union of Geb and Nut. He found consort in his sister Nephthys and the pair unified like their siblings, Osiris and Isis. While his siblings were born naturally by their shared mother, Seth represented disorder immediately upon his arrival into the universe.

Along with his reign over war, Seth was associated with storms, droughts, and the desert. He represented the disorder that is necessary for a balanced universe. His abilities and control over the lands opposed the prosperity and fertility of his older brother, Osiris. They were siblings, but the two gods were eternally at odds with one another from the moment they were born.

Since Greek mythology was influenced so significantly by ancient Egyptian religion, most Egyptian gods and goddesses have a Greek counterpart. Seth's Grecian equivalent is believed to be Typhon, an evil serpent-like god. Typhon is notorious in Greek mythology for his battles against Zeus, the divine equivalent to Ra and, sometimes, Osiris. Unlike in the mythology regarding Seth, Typhon is not believed to have had any redeeming qualities. He was pure evil, inciting terror on Earth and making human beings miserable. Seth, on the other hand, was once a beloved and revered god for many, often being called a hero god.

Seth's True Purpose

Before the atrocities and crimes committed by Seth, which you will learn about in the coming chapters, Seth's purpose in the Great Ennead was to bring chaos and disorder. In order to achieve the ideals of ma'at, the universe must have a balance of good and evil, order and mayhem. This is why it should not come as a surprise that Seth would be such a chaotic force of nature. If the universe was designed by Ra to be a type of utopia, meaning there would be no presence of evil or disorder, the entire concept of ma'at would not exist. Because ma'at is so integral to the ancient Egyptian religion, the pantheon needed to have at least one god that would cause a little negativity.

In the same vein, Seth and Osiris are often viewed as divine examples of order versus chaos. Osiris, who ruled over Egypt as a fair and just king, brought order to the universe. Seth, in contrast, opposed Osiris as often as possible, bringing chaos. This opposition between the two gods is sometimes referred to as the duality of Egyptian mythology and is seen as a necessary aspect of ancient Egyptian religion.

When it comes to Osiris' transition from King of Egypt to King of the Underworld, Seth's role is again seen as necessary. Because of Seth's violence, Osiris was killed and resurrected, forcing him to give up his position as an earthly king. Though he was a well-respected ruler, Osiris' ultimate purpose as a god was to rule over the underworld, protecting the justified dead. If it is to be believed that the gods were fated to their eternal positions, one could argue that Seth was destined to send Osiris to the Underworld to fulfill his destiny. It is entirely possible that, regardless of how brutal Seth's actions were, he had no choice but to complete them in order to maintain the balance of the universe. Otherwise, Osiris would have never become a symbol of resurrection and hope for the people of Egypt.

Chapter 4: Varying Depictions of Seth

Seth's Many Names

Adding to the complex nature and understanding of Seth are the various names and titles he holds. Depending on the source, the god of chaos's name was spelled and pronounced differently. He was commonly referred to as Set, Sutekh, Setekh, Suetekh, Seti, Setesh, and more, in addition to Seth.

Seth has also been granted multiple nicknames throughout history, as told by historians and ancient Egyptians themselves. Partly due to the location of his place of worship and abilities to create droughts, Seth was considered the "Lord of the Desert" (Mark, 2016c). Because the city of Ombos was located south of Lower Egypt, Seth was also called the Ruler of the South.

Even though his existence directly opposed what Osiris was trying to establish as ruler of Egypt, Seth was called upon by humans for many purposes. People would pray to Seth for his protection over their deceased loved ones, in addition to protecting them from his own destruction. He was not often associated with feelings of affection or love, but some sources report Seth's names were inscribed on amulets to create love spells, or on bottles of love potions. The purpose of appealing to the god of chaos regarding love is largely unknown, yet it may be because people were using the spells in his territory. Other beliefs suggest that his strong desire for his sister-wife, Nephthys, was associated with lust, something human beings could evoke in others that they wanted to connect with.

In 1967, Egyptologist and writer Herman te Velde published an analysis of Seth's role in Egyptian mythology. Te Velde dubbed Seth the "God of Confusion," a moniker emphasizing the disorder brought onto the Earth by the deity. The writer goes into detail about the countless other names held by Seth, explaining that the pronunciation and spelling of his name varied depending on the era and territory where it was used in ancient Egypt. In te Velde's book, appropriately named *Seth, God of Confusion*, the etymology behind Seth's name is discussed. An ancient Greek philosopher by the name of Plutarch theorized that Seth's name meant "the overpowering" or "overmastering" (Te Velde, 1967). Herman te Velde refers to Plutarch's theory as pseudo-etymology, as it derives from multiple stories and interpretations, but the author does not discredit the value of Plutarch's knowledge.

The Egyptologist analyzes the other spellings and pronunciations of the god's names and determines that there are at least three distinct meanings at play. After studying the etymology of the various names, te Velde concludes that the Egyptians referred to Seth as an instigator of confusion, deserter, and drunkard.

Other historians and Egyptologists have disagreed with te Velde's use of the phrase "god of confusion." According to some, namely Jan Zandee of the Netherlands, Seth was more than just someone who caused physical and emotional turmoil. The Dutch historian wrote about his opinions about the nickname in a published review of te Velde's book. Instead of calling him a god of confusion, Zandee puts forth the idea of referring to Seth as a god of strength. The god's actions varied between good and evil, sometimes neither, but his strength and might were consistent components in his myths. In a similar review of Herman te Velde's work, Erik Hornung votes to simply call Seth a trickster (Turner, 2012).

With the copious number of names given to Seth throughout history, one thing is for certain: He is a god that does not go unnoticed. His place in Egyptian mythology is solidified for eternity, no matter what he's called—hero-god, trickster, or villain.

Iconography of Seth

Seth may be a god of many titles, but his iconography offers even more ways to view him. The ancient Egyptians depicted Seth through images of animals, mythological creatures, and even human-animal hybrids. Different cities and territories also had specific ways of referring to the god in written language. It is said that there has never been one true image of Seth, due to the countless inconsistencies and interpretations of him across ancient Egypt and beyond.

Like most gods, Seth is associated with certain animals. In his case, however, the list of animals related to his infamy is long. Archaeologists and Egyptologists have found renderings that associate Seth with powerful or aggressive animals, such as the hippopotamus, crocodile, and boar. Some myths suggest the god took the form of venomous animals, due to his destructive nature. This includes serpents and scorpions, the former appearing more frequently in artistic depictions of these myths.

Other less common animals that have been associated with Seth, whether in artistic depictions or written texts, are griffins, tortoises, and donkeys. Griffins have been shown alongside other Seth-related creatures in tomb paintings, appearing in the Tombs of Baqt III and Khety of the 11th Dynasty in Egypt. The griffin is a mythological animal that is considered a composite creature, meaning it has body parts from various animals. The creature is typically described and portrayed with the body, tail, and hind legs of a lion with the wings and head of a falcon or eagle. It is one of many composite creatures that appear throughout Egyptian mythology. Egyptologists assume that the griffin is related to Seth due to its frequent presence in the desert, as well as its addition to several artworks that feature other desert animals. Since Seth is considered Lord of the Desert, it makes sense that he would be associated with most, if not all, desert-living creatures.

There is one mythological creature that is exclusive to Seth, what researchers in modern times have dubbed the Set animal. In ancient Egypt, the being was called a *sha*. The sha is another composite creature made up of multiple animals, depicted with a canine-like body, square ears, and a long snout. It simultaneously resembles a thin dog, aardvark, and giraffe, depending on how it was drawn by ancient artists. With a stiff tail, sometimes forked at the end, and black or red coloring, the sha was a feared creature by many. Red was perceived as a frightening or dangerous color by the Egyptians, so both Seth and the Set animal were commonly depicted with reddish shades on their skin and fur.

An in-depth analysis of varying depictions of the Set animal shows differences in the creature's form. For example, an image of the creature was found on a carving from the second Dynasty, under the rule of the pharaoh Peribsen. In this image, the Set animal has a thick body and short legs. The angle of the animal's neck is measured at 36°, while the angle of its tail is 33°.

In contrast, a second image found of the Set animal from the same time period, but under the rule of the pharaoh Khasekhemwy, has completely different details. The Khasekhemwy carving shows the animal with a lean body and medium-length legs. The neck's angle in this image is measured at 55°, a stark contrast to the first image described. The tail, as well, is set at a different angle, measuring a mere 16°, practically pointed straight up instead of outward like the other image. The final, most significant difference between the two images of the Set animal is that the first carving includes a set of ears, while the second carving shows none (Taylor, 2016).

This type of analysis has been conducted for countless images of both the Set animal and Seth's humanoid forms, resulting in a surplus of data regarding the differing depictions of the god. Researchers have dedicated tens of hours of work to finding out every detail about how Seth was visually represented throughout Egypt.

When he wasn't being portrayed as an animal or composite creature, Seth embodied a more human form. Some artists and philosophers depicted the god of war as a human man with the head of the Set animal. In this form, Seth is known to have carried a *was-scepter,* a long, fork-bottomed staff with the head of an animal on the top end. Seth, of course, carried the head of the sha, or Set animal, on his was-scepter. Additionally, he sometimes took the entire form of a human man, accompanied by the various animals and creatures with whom he is associated.

The Use of Seth's Image in Ancient Egypt

Thousands of years ago, displaying images or artwork that depicted Seth for more than a storytelling purpose was not something to do without forethought. According to research, having an image of Seth in one's temple or tomb would be considered a welcome sign of danger and destruction. Many territories, especially those that worshiped Osiris, believed Seth to be a villain. They would never consider honoring the god by equating his likeness with that of Osiris. Yet, there were a few territories that worshiped Seth, though these places were not as common outside of Upper Egypt.

Eugene Cruz-Uribe writes in his study of Seth that there were circumstances that constituted the use of Seth's image. In his journal article, the Egyptologist describes the discoveries found during the exploration of a temple dedicated to the god Amun, located in Karnak. Archaeologists identified various "Seth figures," meaning images and sculptures of the god, distributed throughout the temple. This discovery suggests that there were cases in which displaying icons of Seth was seen as acceptable. Cruz-Uribe suggests that scribes and artists at the time were not completely against the idea of depicting Seth in sacred venues. Whether the images in the temple were completed before the demonization of Seth or simply regardless of the god's wrongdoings, they remain on the walls of ancient Egyptian buildings.

Cruz-Uribe also determined that Seth was occasionally seen through an ambivalent perspective. Many temples that did not honor the god maintained the idea that he was an equal part of the Egyptian Ennead. Despite his violence and destruction, some members of ancient Egypt viewed him as an integral part of the divine family and subsequent mythology, rather than excluding him from their decorative and historical iconography.

Because of his reputation as a violent and strong god, many of the images depicting Seth show him during battle. Some images portray Seth on the bow of Ra's bark, fending off Apophis. Other images show Seth competing with Horus, the son of Isis and Osiris, for the position of King of Egypt. In these cases, images show Seth and Horus opposing each other in their human-animal hybrid forms; Seth, with the head of the Set animal, and Horus, with the head of a falcon.

Depending on the location of the iconography, Seth would be shown in positions of power or positions of defeat. In one image, discovered in the Tomb of Thaty from the 26th Egyptian

Dynasty, Seth is shown standing behind Horus. Though it appears that both he and Horus are standing in the same position—upright with one hand raised toward their heads—Seth is depicted with four knives stabbing him in various body parts. One in the eye or forehead, another in the back of his skull, a third on the back of his knee, and a fourth in his thigh. It is theorized that the creator of the image begrudgingly included Seth's image but chose to show him being compromised while Horus stands in front of him, uninjured. Analysis of the image states that "although Seth was required in the scene, a decision was made to neutralize him by stabbing him with knives, not the action of a worshipper of Seth" (Taylor, 2016).

During the 2014–2015 reconstruction of the Egyptian Suez Canal, archaeologists discovered a carving of Seth that had never been seen before. On the carving, formally called a *stela*, Seth is standing opposite the Egyptian pharaoh, Ramses I, of the 19th Dynasty. The carving shows the pharaoh making an offering to Seth, who is in his human-animal form (Taylor, 2016). Before the discovery of the stela, it was believed that Ramses was a worshiper of Seth, and the recent discovery of the carving is further proof.

Occasionally, in places where Seth's image alone would raise concern, the god's face was combined with the face of Horus. This type of iconography was often called a depiction of "His Two Faces" (Taylor, 2016). One of these depictions, from the 20th Dynasty, shows one human body dressed in typical Egyptian garb. However, instead of one head at the top of the body, the image shows the head of a Set animal and that of a Horus' falcon. In the image, Seth's animal head is turned at the neck, facing the left, while Horus' head is facing the right.

Another depiction of "His Two Faces," originating from the same dynasty, shows a similar image with three differences.

There is still one human body, accompanied by two heads stemming from the neck. Though, in this depiction, there are four arms outstretched over the body, two on one side and two on the other. As with the first image, Seth's head is facing the left side of the image, and Horus' is facing the right. Unlike the first image described, the body holding the two gods's faces is standing in the middle of a group of six cobras. In addition, the cobras and the gods are balanced on the straight ends of two bows. It is a rather unusual image to imagine, though it is a great example of the fascinating imaginations of ancient artists.

Why Are Depictions of Seth So Inconsistent?

Like most gods, Seth holds many forms and identities. Throughout his mythology, he is represented by various animals and mythological creatures, including combinations of human and animal forms. Because of this, Seth's imagery completely depends on the context in which it has been drawn, as well as the perspective of the artist. For instance, if someone were to be tasked with visually depicting Seth as a desert-bound animal, they would have to choose if he should be shown as a serpent, scorpion, or sha. On top of that, the artist must know the story he is depicting, and whether or not Seth was said to be associated with a specific creature in the context of the story. To make what should be a simple task much more complicated, the artist must know how Seth is viewed in the territory in which the image is being created. If they are drawing an image of Seth for a temple that honors Osiris or Horus, they would most likely need to depict Seth in a way that shows his defeat, rather than make him look like a god worthy of being honored. This can be observed in the image of Seth being stabbed by four knives, while Horus remains unscathed. On the flip side, if the artist were creating the image for a temple that worships Seth, they would have to show him as a formidable, honorable god. Such imagery can be seen in depictions of Seth defeating enemies, such as Apophis, or ruling over the desert.

Another aspect to be considered is how tools, techniques, and mediums changed over the centuries of ancient Egypt's existence. In the earliest years, scribes and artists most likely had limited tools, as well as a virtually blank slate from which to draw inspiration. The first images created to depict Egyptian mythology were based entirely on verbal and written stories. There were no previous drawings or carvings to use as a foundation. Similarly, the mediums on which iconography was drawn changed over time. As new temples and structures were built, more textures and types of stone were available. This, combined with the developing use of colorful paints, most likely changed how artists worked in different eras.

All of these variables make it extremely difficult for Seth's imagery to stay consistent throughout an ever-evolving history.

Chapter 5: Seth, Divine Protector or Evil Incarnate?

Seth the Protector

Before Seth chose to bring mayhem to the universe, he was considered the ultimate protection from evil. With his great strength and knack for violence, the other gods often chose Seth to fend off their enemies. One myth, in particular, gave Seth his initial reputation as being the guardian of Ra, the god of the sun.

To transition the world from day to night, Ra would sail across the globe on his bark, what today would be considered a large sailing ship. According to many interpretations of the myth, Ra would carry the sun with him on his journey. Other interpretations say that the sun itself was Ra's bark. Either way, the Sun God would bring the sun from one side of the Earth to the other, until it was time for the moon to rise. Because the sun's light and warmth were imperative for humanity's survival, Ra's job had to be completed every day, without fail. For a god, it should have been a simple task. However, there were forces at play that were determined to stop the sun from rising each morning.

An evil god named Apophis was the most significant of these forces. He took the form of a massive serpent and represented the harshest components of the universe. Ironically, many of the evils associated with Apophis are also associated with Seth. Darkness, earthquakes, and chaos link the two gods, only separated by a few key differences. Apophis, also known as Apep, Apopis, and Apepi, was a purely malevolent god. He craved death and disorder in a way that Seth did not, fixated on the destruction of the universe and eternal darkness. Seth, on the other hand, has benevolent origins. Though he created earthquakes and droughts, as well as conflict, his purpose as a god in Egyptian mythology is often viewed as a necessary cause of chaos.

To achieve balance and harmony, the key aspects of ma'at, there needed to be a combination of order and chaos. Without chaos, there would be too much order. Alternatively, without order, there would be too much chaos. In the eyes of the Egyptian gods and ancient citizens, the balance of the universe depended on an equal amount of mayhem and peace. This idea is represented by the existence of Seth.

Apophis represented imbalance. Every night, he is said to have plotted the universe's demise. As a god who symbolized darkness, his goal was to defeat Ra and eliminate the sun as a whole. With a world enveloped in the dark, Apophis would be able to ravage humankind easily. On top of that, defeating such a prominent god like Ra would show how powerful the serpent god truly was. For his evil plan to succeed, Apophis would overtake Ra's bark and eliminate the sun god for eternity.

Despite Apophis' tenacity, Ra is not a god known for being easily overthrown. He anticipated the attack and summoned an army to sail with him on his bark. The group consisted of various gods and goddesses, as well as the justified dead—those who died on Earth and were granted eternal life in the Field of Reeds. Seth was one of many deities who fought alongside Ra.

As the sun made its way across the sky, Apophis attacked. Throughout ancient texts and imagery, many gods have been shown defending the sun from the serpent god. Yet it's Seth's role in the fight that is most frequently mentioned. Standing at the front of the bark, Seth is often shown raising a spear against Apophis. Even though different interpretations of the myth reveal multiple gods and goddesses fighting Apophis, Seth is famous for his part in stabbing his enemy in the neck, preventing any further assault on the ship. The moment is seen as a great victory for the deities and humankind.

Unfortunately, Apophis is a god just like any other, meaning he can never truly die. Many myths depicting the brutal battle state that Apophis would merely be slayed for a short time, regenerating throughout the night and coming back the next day to attack Ra's ship again. This cycle would repeat every day as the sun god made his ritual journey. Every day the serpent would attack and, every day, the serpent would be slayed by Seth and his divine family members.

The gods and goddesses were not the only beings to assist Ra in the cyclical battle. In addition to the justified dead who took part in the fight while onboard the bark, men and women on Earth participated in spiritual combat. An ancient text, known today as the Bremner-Rhind Papyrus, details the various rituals and spells performed by ancient Egyptians to protect Ra. The papyrus is filled with instructions for recitation, including threats against Apophis that are referred to as *spells*. One part of the translated text reads: "Thou art fallen, driven off and turned back, O Apep...Horus has repelled thy rage, Seth has rendered thy moment (of action) impotent" (Faulkner, 1937). This phrase, which is believed to have been recited by the ancient people during their ritual, is followed by pages and pages of additional spells. The ancient Egyptians had a strong belief that, by reciting such spells, Apophis would be weakened, and Ra's army would have more success defeating him. Other parts of the humans' ritual include spitting on figures of Apophis and destroying his images, typically by burning them in a fire (Mark, 2017b).

Sometimes, the sun was overtaken by the enemy, or so the ancient Egyptians believed. In the occasional event of a solar eclipse, during which the sun is blocked by the moon and mostly hidden for those on Earth, the ancient people would worry that Apophis had succeeded in his attack. Thankfully for the Egyptians, Seth would defeat him once again the next day.

Likely because of Seth's protection, it has been observed by researchers that Ra took a liking to the god. In "The Contendings of Horus and Seth," a mythological story written in another ancient Egyptian papyrus, Ra often provides comfort to Seth after any lost battles or failures. It is also said that Ra "adopted" Seth and invited him to live with the sun god in the sky (Rikala, 2007). Even after Seth's future crimes, Ra continued to support his grandson and allow him a place in the cosmos.

The World's First Murderer

Despite his original status as a hero, Seth could not avoid his penchant for mayhem. Along with his destructive nature, the god was known for becoming extremely jealous of those who had what he did not. This jealousy eventually caused him to commit a crime that would alter the roles of the gods for eternity. But before going into detail, it's important to discuss the events leading up to his transgression.

When the Great Ennead was established, the gods and goddesses separated themselves into couples. The children of Geb and Nut paired off, Isis becoming the sister-wife of Osiris and Nephthys becoming the sister-wife of Seth. Osiris and Isis are commonly viewed as the more powerful duo, though Seth and Nephthys held significant power of their own. Nephthys, specifically, had magical abilities that she would use to her advantage.

One myth describes the Nephthys' use of magic to fool Osiris. Because she and Seth never had their own child, the goddess saw an opportunity to conceive without her brother-husband. Nephthys utilized her powers to transform her physical appearance, turning herself into a replica of Isis. Disguised as her sister, the goddess sought out Osiris, knowing he would not be able to tell her true identity. Nephthys tricked Osiris into having a child with her, whom she would later name Anubis. Both Seth and Isis were enraged at the unfaithfulness of their consorts. Despite Osiris being an unwilling partner in the adultery, the betrayal triggered the first bout of Seth's jealousy and anger toward his brother.

Leading up to, and during, the affair between Nephthys and Osiris, the latter was establishing his place as Egypt's first king. He was beloved by the ancient Egyptians and worshiped all over the country. Osiris was said to be a fair but generous king, offering everything humans needed to survive on Earth. Naturally, Seth grew jealous of his brother's position. The god of chaos desired the power that Osiris held over Egypt and the worship he received in return. That jealousy, coupled with the growing resentment of his brother for having a child with his wife, became too strong for Seth to ignore.

Seth saw only one possible way to take his brother's place on the throne. Osiris must be eliminated. Seth formed a vicious plan to trick Osiris into abandoning his role as king. As the myth describes, Seth plotted to build a large chest, big enough for his brother's body, in which he would lock Osiris and send him down the Nile River to drown. It is said that Seth sneaked into Osiris' bedroom while the king was sleeping and took precise measurements of his body. The god of chaos brought the measurements to a carpenter, who built a beautifully ornate wooden chest covered in colorful paint and plaques of gold.

After the chest was built, Seth summoned his friends and family members to his home for a celebration, inviting Osiris as the guest of honor. The festivities raged on throughout the night, but Seth was focused on his plan. He told the attendees that he had created a game. Whoever could fit perfectly inside his new wooden chest would be allowed to keep it as their own. One after another, Seth's partygoers attempted to fit themselves into the container, though no one was a perfect fit. Knowing that the chest was created with Osiris' exact measurements, Seth called on his brother to try his hand at the game. Osiris, being a powerful god who would never deny a challenge, climbed into the chest with vigor. As expected, he fit perfectly inside. Seth proceeded to close the chest around Osiris and lock it tightly, preventing the king from escaping. Seth and his friends carried the chest to the riverbank and pushed it into the water. Osiris was defeated.

With no king to claim the throne of Egypt, Seth took his opportunity with pride. For a short time, he ruled over the land, despite the grief felt by the ancient Egyptians for their former king. When Isis got word of her husband's disappearance, she scoured the Nile for the wooden chest. The goddess eventually found it and tore it open, only to reveal her husband's dead body. Isis wept for Osiris and grew furious at her brother, Seth, knowing he was to blame. However, she knew that there were rituals that could bring her husband back to life. The rituals required precision and the proper tools, so Isis hid Osiris' limp body in the grassy area beside the riverbank while she went to collect what she needed.

While Isis was gone, Seth arrived at the Nile to ensure the wooden chest and his brother's body were successfully washed away. He found no evidence of either in the river's waters, a realization that caused him to check the surrounding areas. Seth searched the tall grass alongside the river and, much to his dismay, found his brother's body. Seething, Seth took a sharp knife and cut Osiris' body into pieces. Surely, this would make it impossible for anyone to revive the former king. Seth scattered the pieces of his brother's body across Egypt. Seth was satisfied with his work and, once again, claimed his place on the Egyptian throne.

Upon her return to the riverbank, Isis was unable to find Osiris in the grass. She knew Seth must have found her husband and done something even more sinister to him. Using her divine powers, Isis transformed herself into a bird and soared across the country in search of Osiris. She found the fragmented pieces of his body and brought them back to her territory. With the help of her sister, Nephthys, and nephew, Anubis, Osiris' body was put back together. The deities wrapped the body in linen and performed a sacred ritual that would bring Osiris back to life. The ritual was successful, thanks to the magical abilities of both Isis and Nephthys, and Osiris was alive once more.

Interpretations of the myth of Osiris' revival vary, though most agree that it was at this moment that Isis conceived her and her husband's first child, Horus. Sadly, Osiris was not able to celebrate the conception for long. Because he had died and gone to the Duat, it was his duty to return and become King of the Afterlife. From then on, Osiris was seen as a symbol of hope and life after death, while Isis and the Nile River were praised for their powers of resurrection. Furthermore, Seth was seen as the world's first murderer.

Seth Versus Horus

After the brutal murder and consequential dethroning of Osiris, Seth gained many enemies. The most significant of these enemies was Horus, son of Isis and Osiris. Like she did with her husband's dead body, Isis hid her son from Seth after his birth. Isis knew that Horus was the true heir to the Egyptian throne, meaning he was a threat to Seth even at his young age.

The goddess kept Horus hidden away until he was old enough to avenge his father's displacement. In "The Contendings of Horus and Seth," the lengthy competition between the two gods is described. The papyrus detailing the competition is considered one of the only complete stories in ancient Egypt (Rikala, 2007). According to the story, Seth and Horus continually battled each other for the position of king. Many of these battles were nonviolent, instead based on trickery and trivial contests. "The Contendings of Horus and Seth" papyrus was written with a more humorous tone than other ancient texts, and the stories about the gods' competitions are rather surprising.

The opposition between the two gods was well-known among the other divine beings. All of the gods and goddesses were tasked with deciding who would take Osiris' place as king. Seth had the strength and will to defeat all of Egypt's enemies, but Horus was the son of the former king and could extend his father's great legacy. Seth also held many more years of experience over Horus, engaging in a lifetime of combat and protecting Ra against Apophis. Alternatively, Horus was favored by the gods who loved Osiris. In order to decide who would become ruler, the gods and goddesses of ancient Egypt spent over 80 years watching Horus and Seth compete with one another. The following stories are taken from various interpretations of "The Contendings of Horus and Seth":

Isis' Intervention

Because the battle between Seth and Horus had been going on for so long, the gods and goddesses tasked with crowning the next king decided to bring the contest to a new location. Simply put, they were growing bored of the long-lasting competition. Those involved in the contest, including the contenders and judges, set off on a ferryboat to a distant island. Here, they would continue their games and battles until a king was finally chosen.

Because she had a vendetta against her brother, Isis was not allowed to travel to the island. The judges worried her presence would tip the scales unfairly in her son's favor due to her magical abilities and desire for revenge. So, believing they left Isis behind on the mainland, the group sailed toward the island.

Isis was more determined than ever to help her son. Using magic, she disguised herself as a poor, old, human woman. Before the ship set sail, she made her way onto the boat and convinced the captain to let her join the trip with the other men and women on board. The captain knew he was forbidden from allowing Isis on the ship, but for all he knew, this was an ordinary woman seeking refuge and adventure. He generously let her sail to the island with the rest of the group.

Once the ship arrived at its destination, Isis transformed again, this time disguising herself as a beautiful, young woman. She located Seth before the contest and told him a fabricated story. Isis convinced Seth that she was a young, widowed mother, taking care of her only son. She told the god that a strange man had stolen her property, as well as evicted her son from their shared home. The goddess must have been quite convincing, as Seth believed her lies and agreed that the "strange man" was in the wrong. While Isis condemned the fictional stranger for his arrogance and theft, Seth did, too. In doing so, he had been fooled into indirectly condemning himself, as he had committed the same atrocities as the man Isis was chastising.

Upon hearing what she wanted Seth to say, Isis transformed back into her goddess self. She reveled in the fact that she had proven to the judges, once and for all, that Seth was an unworthy choice for king of Egypt. Seth understood his mistake and challenged Horus to a duel, postponing the judges' decision once more. This duel was known by some ancient Egyptians as the Great Quarrel.

The Great Quarrel

The duel between Seth and Horus took place at the Nile River, the place of origin for the initial opposition between the two gods. This was where Seth had killed Osiris years prior, igniting the hatred and vengeance that had built up in Horus. The Nile was also where Isis had discovered her husband's deceased form. It was a location that brought up intense emotions for all of the gods and goddesses.

At the river, Seth and Horus were instructed to fight each other, but with an interesting twist. Both gods would have to transform into hippopotamuses and engage in combat underwater. In addition, the fight would last up to three months. The first hippopotamus to breach the surface of the water would lose the fight. Agreeing, Seth and Horus transformed into the deadly creatures and met each other in the river.

According to the myth, Isis watched the ensuing battle from the riverbank. Still furious at Seth for his many tricks and crimes, she devised another plan to prevent him from winning. The goddess threw a harpoon into the river, aiming for Seth's hippopotamus form. To her surprise and frustration, Isis accidentally lodged the harpoon into her own son's body. She quickly used her magic to remove the harpoon and attempted, a second time, to slay Seth. Her second throw was aimed perfectly, stabbing Seth and injuring him.

Though her interference was a success in Isis' eyes, her son was angered by her meddling. Horus emerged from the Nile in a fit of rage, searching for his mother. The young god attacked Isis and tore her head from her body. The reaction was an unnecessary use of violence, the exact trait of Seth's that Horus hated. Horus is said to have regretted his decision instantly and fled the scene, carrying his mother's decapitated head with him. He sought out the god Thoth who replaced Isis' head with that of a cow. The image of the cattle-headed goddess can often be found in Isis' iconography.

In an unexpected change of character, Seth wanted to seek revenge on his nephew for the brutalization of his sister. He found Horus and ripped his eyes out of his head, rendering him completely and utterly blind. As with Isis' injury, Horus was able to be healed by Thoth and regained his eyesight soon enough.

Nevertheless, regardless of the brief moment of familial love between Seth and Isis after her decapitation, the gods were still at odds with one another. Isis forgave her son for his attack and Seth continued to fight for his role as king.

Another conflict between Seth and Horus is told through a graphic tale of deception. Oddly enough, the story behind the conflict involves sexual assault, bodily emissions, and contaminated lettuce. It is both a fascinating and unusual tale that could only come from the vivid storytelling of the ancient Egyptians.

After the Great Quarrel, the gods and goddesses in charge of crowning the new king became overwhelmed by the chaos that the contests had caused. Everyone involved in the battles was summoned back to the judges' court, where a banquet would be held in celebration of their safe return home. Perhaps the banquet was an attempt at easing the tension between the gods and alleviating the growing stress.

During the celebration, Horus became intoxicated by the many drinks being served. Seth convinced the younger god to go to sleep, having hatched one more plan to defeat his nephew. While Horus slept off his drunken stupor, Seth mounted him, as a man would a woman. Seth attempted to shame Horus by filling him with his seed, proving that Seth truly was the more powerful god. What he did not expect, however, was for Horus to have a plan of his own. The latter had faked his drunkenness, knowing Seth would try to take advantage of his vulnerability. When Seth completed his assault, Horus caught the emissions instead of letting them enter his body. He removed himself from beneath Seth's body and ran to Isis, revealing to her what Seth had done. Isis took Horus' tainted hand and amputated it, ridding her son of Seth's contamination.

Afterward, Isis had Horus produce his own seed into a jar, which she promptly brought to the nearby vegetable garden. Isis asked the gardener which vegetables were most favored by Seth. The gardener told the goddess that the only vegetable Seth would eat was lettuce, prompting Isis to throw the jar into the growing crop of lettuce, thus contaminating it with her son's emissions. Later on, Seth ingested a head of lettuce and became pregnant with Horus' seed.

The two gods hurried to the judges to explain their sides of the conflict, with Seth stating that he had bested Horus by overpowering him and filling him with his seed. Horus, in turn, revealed that he had tricked Seth and told the judges about the contaminated lettuce, therefore proving that it was he who had bested Seth once and for all. The gods and goddesses of the court declared that Horus was correct, he had finally gotten the better of the god of chaos.

Seth, though, had one more plan to put into action. He convinced the judges to allow one more competition before they made their decision. Whether the judges were enjoying their ongoing entertainment, or simply because Seth had charmed them, the last competition was scheduled.

The Boat Race

The final battle described in the ancient papyrus tells the tale of a boat race between the two gods. Unlike many other interpretations of Seth, this story describes him as an easily tricked and gullible fool. There are several versions of the tale told by different interpreters, although the outcomes are all the same.

Seth organized the race, explaining that he and Horus would have to construct a vessel to race across the river. The winner of the race would be granted kingship. However, researchers have discovered that Seth's instructions could be interpreted in two different ways. One interpretation indicates that the vessels should be made *of* stone, while the second interpretation states they should be made *for* stone, meaning the ability to carry stones across the river (Taylor, 2016). The case of the double meaning is said to either be a play on words or simply a miscommunication on Seth's part.

As the story goes, Horus and Seth got to work building their vessels, forming them into small ships. Seth followed the first interpretation of the rules, carving his boat out of stone. Horus, on the other hand, decided to follow the second interpretation. He built his boat out of wood, ensuring that it was lightweight and able to sail swiftly. Knowing Seth would notice the difference in materials, Horus painted his vessel to mirror the look of stone. He was able to convince Seth that the boats were of equal weight and substance. When the race began, Seth's boat sank almost immediately, while the boat made by Horus sailed on without issue.

The gods and goddesses judging the competition viewed Seth as a fool, having been bested by his young opponent. Supporters of Seth, though, acknowledged Horus' trickery and claimed he was a cheater, undeserving of being crowned king. Seth was furious at his nephew for tricking him and, again, turned himself into a hippopotamus and dove into the water. He destroyed Horus' boat with the aggression and violence for which he was infamous. Osiris, who had been watching the decades-long battle between his brother and son from the Underworld, finally spoke up and told the judges to put an end to the competitions.

Osiris decided it would be his son, Horus, who would take his place on the Egyptian throne. Seth, finally defeated, was sent to reside alongside Ra and protect the sun god from enemies.

The Duality of Seth and Horus

The contention between Seth and Horus provides more than just entertaining myths. Much like Seth's relationship with his brother Osiris, he and Horus represent a balance between chaos and order. The two gods are a divine example of the duality of Egyptian mythology. Throughout the aforementioned myths, Seth created chaos by continuously trying to overpower Horus with his trickery and strength. Horus, despite his own deception of Seth and violence against his mother, represented the fight for order. His goal was to follow in his father's footsteps and reign as a just, generous king. If Seth were to be king, Egypt would most likely be caught in endless battles and conflicts.

In a way, Seth's failure to take Osiris' place on the throne is a result of his true purpose as an Egyptian god. He was created to bring necessary evil to the world, to find balance with the order. He represents the eternal conflict of human beings in which they have to find their own balance of good and evil. When Osiris ruled over Egypt, he was Seth's equal counterpart. When he was sent to rule over the Underworld, Horus replaced him and continued to maintain the balance with Seth. Alone, Seth would bring too much chaos to the universe. With Horus as his opponent, the two would forever be balanced on opposite sides of the metaphorical scale. Together, they represent the importance of ma'at.

Chapter 6: Seth's Influence on Culture

Regardless of his violent and deceptive reputation, Seth was worshiped in various places across Egypt. There have been many pharaohs who associated themselves with the god of chaos, even giving themselves names that were inspired by Seth. In some cases, those who worshiped Seth honored his strength and devotion to the sun god, Ra. These worshipers saw past the violent acts and saw Seth in a positive light. In other cases, the violence and deception were the reasons why Seth was worshiped. Depending on the intentions of the cult or pharaoh, Seth was seen as a hero or as a fearsome force of power.

Even after ancient Egypt evolved into a more contemporary society, Seth's name and reputation as a god were used as the building blocks for certain cults. His influence was also not restricted to Egypt's barriers, as is seen in the establishment of a 1970s American cult.

To fully understand Seth's long-lasting influence, one must begin by acknowledging the ancient rulers and territories that kept Seth's legacy alive.

Places of Worship

Seth was mostly worshiped in Upper Egypt which, ironically, was located more toward the southern point of the country. The god's reign even extended as far as the dry, barren desert on the borders of Egypt, establishing his influence over foreign lands and civilizations. The oases within the desert lands were the location of various cities and civilizations, most of whom worshiped Seth for his ability to control the deserts and storms.

In ancient times, Seth was considered the patron of the 11th division of Egypt, more specifically in the city of Nubt, also called Ombos. The city was located on the western riverbank of the Nile and was considered a highly populated area due to the discovery of its vast cemeteries. Ombos is believed to be the first location to worship Seth in ancient Egypt.

Other desert oases associated with the worship of Seth are the Kharga Oasis, the Dakhla Oasis, and the Siwa Oasis. Each of these locations held several sites where Seth's iconography has been discovered. In Dakhla, as many as six different areas are known to be connected to Seth. The Kharga Oasis also had at least two Seth-worshiping areas, while the Siwa Oasis had at least one (Taylor, 2016).

The Temples of Edfu and Dendera, both located in Upper Egypt, hold concrete evidence of the worship of Seth. Archaeologists and Egyptologists have discovered carvings of the god's iconography dating back to around 57 B.C.E (Taylor, 2016).

Another location in the now-lost ancient town of Sepermeru, honored Seth with a temple named the House of Seth, Lord of Sepermeru. Within the temple were shrines dedicated to Seth and Nephthys, honoring both the god of chaos and his sister-wife. The town of Sepermeru has also been dubbed "the gateway to the desert," of which Seth was considered the ultimate ruler (Wikipedia, 2023).

The Hyksos People

Around 1780 B.C.E, a group of people called the Hyksos came to Egypt. The ancient Egyptians were not threatened by the invasion and the new community made their home in Avaris, located near the northeastern riverbank of the Nile. Here, the Hyksos people accustomed themselves to the ways of ancient Egyptians, donning Egyptian clothing and learning the customs of their new land. Unlike many invaders that would later take advantage of Egyptian civilization, the Hyksos collaborated with the ancient Egyptians and put them in positions of high power and importance.

The newcomers already worshiped gods from their homeland, but, in their assimilation to Egyptian culture, they found commonalities between their beloved gods and those of the ancient Egyptian religion. They associated their storm god, Baal, with Seth, choosing to honor Seth as they would Baal in their place of origin. Additionally, the Hyksos people viewed hippopotamuses as sacred creatures, due to their association with Seth. During the Hyksos's time in Egypt, it is said that "trade flourished" and there was no animosity between the new community and the surrounding territories (Mark, 2017a).

Sadly, the Hyksos territory was all but destroyed when the Theban army ravaged their land and burned their buildings to the ground.

The Abandonment of Seth's Influence

As the ancient Egyptians's beliefs about religion evolved, the number of Seth's places of worship lessened. In what is often called the demonization of Seth, led by newer interpretations of the murder of Osiris, Seth began to be seen as a villain instead of a necessary evil. New pharaohs were repulsed by the idea of worshiping such a god, and Seth's iconography was stripped from many of the locations in which it had once been featured. His reputation fluctuated throughout the progression of ancient Egypt, further complicating his mythological legacy.

Nonetheless, the desert oases that worshiped Seth continued to honor him. They were not repulsed by his actions, but, if they were, it was not enough to stop them from worshiping the god that protected their land.

Pharaohs Who Worshiped Seth

There were a handful of Egyptian pharaohs who worshiped the god of chaos. Ramses I, who also went by the name Ramesses I, founded the 19th Dynasty of Egyptian rulers. As discussed in Chapter 4, Ramses I is depicted in an image with Seth, making an offering to the god. This finding is concrete evidence that the pharaoh, who only ruled for a few short years, honored Seth. Rather than exclude Seth's imagery and ideals from his kingdom, Ramses I chose to not only create new depictions of Seth, but also include himself as a worshiper. By portraying himself in this way, Ramses I solidified his approval of and devotion to Seth.

In addition to honoring the god of chaos through his iconography, Ramses I associated Seth with his family. After the birth of his son, Ramses I chose to name the baby Seti. The name translates to "of Set," formally linking the young prince with the controversial god. Seti was raised to be a ruler like his father and, once of age, became a joint ruler alongside Ramses I. The father and son duo reportedly reigned over Egypt from 1290 to 1279 B.C.E (Britannica, 2023c).

Seti was a king who desired a better reputation for Egypt. In the years leading up to his reign, Egypt is said to have lost its great prestige. Seti was determined to bring the country back to its former glory, battling whichever armies stood in his way. His connection with Seth was further solidified by his willingness to use violence in battle, along with his desire to protect the integrity of his kingdom.

This connection to the god of chaos was restricted, however. As Seti rebuilt tombs and rectified decaying buildings across Egypt, he dedicated his work to Osiris, Seth's eternal opponent. Seti linked himself to Osiris by building not one, but two buildings of worship in the god's honor.

Seth's Contemporary Influence

Temple of Set

Although most people today do not worship the Egyptian gods, at least not in the same way as the ancient Egyptians, it was not too long ago that a cult was formed in honor of Seth. In 1966, a community called the Church of Satan was established in the United States. Satan, the devil who plagues religions such as Judaism, Christianity, and Islam, is commonly known as the devil. The members of the Church of Satan, however, did not worship the actual satanic entity. The founding member, Anton LaVey, created the group's manifesto, titled *The Satanic Bible*. Along with the rituals and teachings of his church, LaVey clarified the meaning behind the use of the name Satan. The Church of Satan's leader declared that he and his members worshiped the overarching idea of Satan as a symbol of rebellion, self-assertion, and personal strength. It is reported that there were a few thousand members of the Church of Satan in its prime.

In 1975, less than 10 years after the Church of Satan's formation, one of its most important members abandoned LaVey's teachings. Michael Aquino, who worked closely with LaVey during his time in the Church, decided to create his own community. Aquino named his new cult the Temple of Set, a tongue-in-cheek salute to his former church.

Upon creation of his new cult, Aquino claimed to have been visited by Seth in a dream. The Egyptian god supposedly dictated to Aquino what would later become the manifesto of the Temple of Set. It is reported that the cult had around 110 members across the country, thousands fewer than the Church of Satan (Van Zak, 1976). These members were said to be allowed into Aquino's cult if they followed three specific steps.

First, they must acknowledge the problematic nature of organized religions, as well as the lacking beliefs of atheism and agnosticism. Secondly, any potential member must have a true desire to connect with and learn more about Seth. Finally, incoming members were required to pay a $37 membership fee in order to participate in the activities of the Temple of Set. Aquino named his cult members "Setians" (Van Zak, 1976).

The Setians had very few organized activities and duties, but they were sure to honor Seth during the nighttime when darkness fell over the country. Presumably, this idea was put into place because of Seth's association with darkness and storms. The members of Aquino's cult believed that nighttime was the only time to connect with their god, who represented true rebellion and religious anarchy.

Setians also worshiped Set by performing rituals that they believed were magical. Using pentagrams and a strong will, Aquino and his associates attempted to use magic to alter the laws of the universe, much like Seth had done throughout his mythology. The ritual was performed by the Setians with enthusiasm, according to a newspaper article written about the cult in 1976. The cult members were eager to bend the universe to their will, through the power of Seth.

It is clear that Seth's reputation inspired many communities and groups of people throughout history, creating connections between ancient civilizations and modern cults that may have otherwise never been linked. The god of chaos' legacy not only provides entertaining stories and moral intrigue but a lasting impression on those who choose to identify with the complex god.

Chapter 7: Man's Moral Struggles Mirror Seth's Legacy

Jealousy, anger, and the desperate desire for total control are just a few of the themes that circulate the stories about Seth. Though the tales you read about the god are rather unique, the messages behind them are often found in the lives of humans throughout history. Undoubtedly, every human being has experienced the complex emotions portrayed in Seth's myths, in one way or another. Of course, a human may not trick their older brother into climbing into a casket and sending him down the Nile River, but a human certainly has times when they will do whatever it takes to gain total control over a situation.

Being in a position of great power can affect people differently. Someone's personality, lifestyle, and personal circumstances can alter how they handle their position. All too often, humanity has shown that power belongs in the hands of some and should be kept far away from the hands of others. Although, it all comes down to the concept of morality.

Human Morality Is Not Black and White

Everyone has their own opinion on what it means to have good morals. Some people say that being a kind and generous person shows that a person has a strong moral conscience. Parents tell their young children to "play nice," hoping the sentiment will stay ingrained in the child's mind for life. Few parents, for instance, want their kids to be bullies, so they teach them about morality from a young age.

The issue with morality is that it is not black and white. What sets humans apart from other species is our ability to think about the future, plan our actions far in advance, and consider the consequences. This special trait of ours means that we all have varying opinions, especially concerning good versus evil. It would be nice to imagine that all people believe that murder is bad and that saving lives is good. With morality being completely subjective, however, these idealistic belief systems are put up for debate.

What if someone is murdered out of self-defense? Is it still considered evil to protect oneself? On the other side of the spectrum, what if saving someone's life meant harming someone else? Would it be viewed as morally right? Take this classic hypothetical, for example, a person steals a loaf of bread to feed their starving family. They are aware that theft is illegal, or simply viewed as morally wrong, but their family would have died of starvation without the bread.

There are numerous arguments to be made here, on both the side of the law and the side of the starving family. One could argue that no one should commit a crime, such as theft, no matter what their personal situation is. Another person could retaliate with the idea that the right thing to do is feed a family in need, outweighing the minor inconvenience of a stolen loaf of bread. A third person, feeling rather ambiguous, could suggest that the person could have stolen the bread, fed their family, and then given themselves up to the authorities for committing a crime. Such moral debates could continue for hours without a unanimously satisfying solution, all because people have different moral standards. It is when a person takes their moral stance and acts in self-interest, to the extent in which they cause harm or destruction to others, that moral gray areas become a problem.

American theologian, Reinhold Niebuhr, wrote an entire book about the complexity of man's struggle with morality, titled *Moral Man and Immoral Society: A Study in Ethics and Politics*. The book was originally published in 1932, however, it touches on aspects of society that are still true in the 21st century. Much of his writing centers around the convoluted dynamic between politics and morality. As has been proven consistently in political controversies, many people with high government titles have been accused of immoral acts, like corruption and white-collar crime. Relying on moral integrity alone has been shown to not matter as much as a politician's social status, connections, and bank account. Niebuhr expands on this idea in his book and questions the power of good morals against social and economic injustices.

Speaking on the concept of human selfishness, Niebuhr writes that "there are definite limits in the capacity of ordinary mortals which makes it impossible for them to grant to others what they claim for themselves" (Niebuhr, 2017). Essentially, the author believes that human beings have a limit to how much they can do for others out of goodwill, or the hope for world peace. He adds that a high level of intelligence and moral understanding can increase a person's capacity for selflessness, but not enough to make them put another person over themselves in every single scenario. Presumably, the types of scenarios Niebuhr is referring to are those of life and death, or another life-changing opportunity. However, the writer's ideas can be challenged by the notion of someone sacrificing themselves for a loved one, or those who put their lives in danger to protect their nations.

Niebuhr also shares his opinions on the idea of love being a driving force behind social benevolence and morality. His writing indicates his belief that being a *good person*, one who acts in kindness and goodwill, will never be powerful enough to stop social injustices or corruption. The author reminds readers that all large-scale collectives, such as governments and communities, must rely on a fair amount of coercion to stay unified. Rarely is there a large group of people that can all agree on everything. There will always be outliers that disagree with the majority, even if the majority is working in the best interest of the collective. As Niebuhr says, these groups must be coerced and manipulated, to a degree, in order to maintain a stable community or government. A true utopia, where everyone is in sync and there are no moral disagreements, is merely a pipe dream.

When it comes to one person or entity holding immense power over another, morality becomes even harder to pin down. In many Western societies, there are multiple levels of government leaders to distribute power more equally. In the United States, for example, a president is elected to be the head of the country, but he must work together with the other branches of the Federal Government. The three levels belonging to the US government are the legislative, executive, and judicial branches. Essentially, there is the President and his consorts, the Congress, and the Federal Courts. For the most part, this allows for decisions on behalf of the country to be made by multiple people, rather than one.

The founders of the United States of America recognized the potential for corruption if the fate of the country were to be in the hands of one person. They understood that moral strength has its limits and that something significant enough could cause a person to lose sight of their values. If that were to happen, a country without a balanced power dynamic could fall victim to a dangerous dictatorship. Thus, the three branches of government were formed.

In ancient Egypt, power dynamics were not as difficult to balance. The gods were the ultimate source of control, giving humankind the tools for survival in return for their worship. Below the gods were the kings, said to be chosen by the divine beings themselves, making it hard for anyone to argue about. Then there were the citizens: noblemen, scribes, priests, and the lower classes. Due to their strong beliefs in their religion, few people tried to break from their predestined roles. Apart from the few who lived life in opposition to the gods' and goddesses' moral laws, everyone in ancient Egypt was determined to live well enough and without conflict to earn eternal residence in the Field of Reeds.

Power Has Always Controlled Man

It has been observed for centuries; a person or organization gains a significant amount of power and suddenly becomes corrupt. Maybe they gained enough societal importance to be listened to without question, causing them to take advantage of the situation before them. Maybe they got a taste of what it is like to feel superior over another, giving them an unfaltering sense of being invincible. It happens all the time, even under the most trivial circumstances.

Imagine a typical American high school, like the ones often depicted in television shows and movies. A lonely, impressionable teenager feels ostracized and alienated. Despite their efforts, the teenager feels that they truly do not belong. They get ignored by their classmates, overlooked by the person they have a crush on, and laughed at by the popular kids.

Then, one day, something happens, and they finally befriend the kids that once laughed at them. They begin to associate with the crowd of popular students, quickly gaining a reputation for being one of the *cool kids*. Other students look at them with envy and awe. Everything finally feels fun and exciting. The once-ignored teen feels the satisfaction of being popular. Over time, they too start laughing at other students, turning their nose up at those who don't have such a high social status. They have been corrupted by the power of feeling superior to their peers.

But why *does* power corrupt people so fiercely? An article published in the Smithsonian Magazine digs deeper into the question, analyzing the science behind what causes a person to succumb to the negative side effects of power. The article describes a study conducted by psychologists that tested adults' moral identities against opportunities to have power. Here, moral identity is defined as "the degree to which [the adults] thought it was important to their sense of self to be 'caring,' 'compassionate,' 'fair,' 'generous' and so on" (Shea, 2012). Basically, one's moral identity is based on how they view being a good person. The results of the study showed that people with higher moral identity, meaning those who find it important to be morally good, are more likely to use power to benefit the collective group. Those with lower moral identity, as in those who cared less about being morally good, used power to benefit themselves, with little to no concern about the rest of the group.

What this study truly means is that there is a significant possibility that morality, in an objective sense, can affect how someone uses their access to power. Someone who does not identify "good morals" with being generous, compassionate, and fair, is likely the type of person who will be corrupted by power. These types of people have consistently appeared throughout human history.

The Battle of the Pyramids

In 1798, French dictator Napoleon Bonaparte took his military to Egypt intending to capture Cairo, the country's capital city. The reason behind Napoleon's invasion was two-fold: gaining control of Egypt would provide France with an increase in income, in addition to keeping England from its most significant source of imported goods, effectively destroying the country's financial stability. Thus, the French military eagerly invaded Egypt.

At the time of the invasion, Egypt was under the control of the Ottoman Empire. Napoleon Bonaparte told the Egyptian people that he would free them from unjust Ottoman rule, though his true plan was to take Egypt from the Ottoman Empire and put the country under French control. During Bonaparte's invasions, Egyptian citizens were displaced and left to suffer, some even being slaughtered as a result of the ensuing violence. The invasion and subsequent war between the French military and the Ottoman-controlled Egyptian army became known as the Battle of the Pyramids.

Napoleon urged his troops to ravage the Egyptian army's camp, causing mayhem. The Egyptian soldiers were dispersed by the French, running for their lives to the only place that was not surrounded by French troops: the Nile River. Many of those who fled to the river drowned.

It is said that, by the end of the Battle of the Pyramids, up to 6,000 Egyptians had been killed, either by drowning or by violence (Britannica, 2023b). Ultimately, Napoleon and his army were defeated and forced out of Egypt, but not without severe detriment to the Egyptian people.

Napoleon Bonaparte has been called a military genius and advocate for religious freedom. However, he has also been described as a "power-hungry dictator," "tyrant," and a "proud, vain man" (Tousignant, 2021). His deep desire for control over the Eastern hemisphere led to the deaths of millions of people, including innocent civilians. He had an obsession with power that caused him to believe he could control the world with his military. Yet, to this day, many of his conquests are seen as successes, despite the damage they caused. One could argue his moral identity was not tied to the ideals of being fair, generous, or compassionate. Instead, he likely viewed himself as a hero of France, connecting his moral identity with what benefited him and his own people.

Historical Dictatorship

With moral identities similar to Napoleon, dictators in other Western countries rose to power. In the 20th century, men by the names of Adolf Hitler and Joseph Stalin caused history-making destruction as a result of their deep-seated desire for power. These dictators have made such an impact on humanity that their devastating legacies are still taught in schools all over the world. Hitler and Stalin are commonly known as the most infamous totalitarian leaders of the 1900s.

German dictator, Adolf Hitler, is credited with starting World War II after he began invading surrounding countries. At the time, Germany was in an unfortunate state of unrest and desperation due to their humiliating loss in the first World War. Germany was forced to pay reparations for the damage it had caused in the war, which significantly hurt their economy. In the late 1930s, Hitler rose to power quickly, convincing the German people that he would bring their country back to greatness. However, his intentions were not pure. The dictator took advantage of his country's desperate need for a strong leader and became an unflinching force of evil. He represented a toxic amount of nationalism and racism, believing that only people with specific genetics deserved to inhabit Western society.

Hitler's Nazi army invaded several European countries, including Poland, Denmark, and France, among others (United States Holocaust Memorial Museum, 2019). He killed millions of people, particularly those of the Jewish faith and people of color. His superiority complex and need for total control ignited the most devastating world war in history. For those who believe in equality and justice for all people, regardless of their identities, Hitler's crusades were the ultimate act of evil. He went against all sound morals and became consumed with his power over the world. Fortunately, he was finally defeated and exiled from his homeland, but he left behind a horrifying legacy of dictatorship.

Around the same time as Hitler's rise to power came the dictatorship of Joseph Stalin in the Soviet Union, now known as

Russia. Stalin had wild ideas of transforming the Soviet Union into an economic and military superpower, which he planned to achieve through a dictatorship based on communism. The tyrant began by forcing landowners and farmers out of their homes and sending them to concentration camps. His goal was to collect every farm in the Soviet Union and put them under the government's control, thus giving himself total power over the country's agriculture. If the landowners and farmers resisted his orders, they were arrested and, as was often the case, murdered by his military.

In addition to killing any civilians who opposed him, Stalin eliminated any military soldiers who chose to speak out against his rule. It is said that over three million members of Soviet Union society were arrested and sent to Siberian labor camps. To make matters worse, around 750,000 of these people were killed during the process (BBC, 2019).

Eventually, Stalin and Hitler became allies in the destruction of humanity. The two dictators agreed to split up the countries they had invaded and wished to invade in the future, while forming a pact that would protect Germany from the Soviet Union and vice versa. Unsurprisingly, Hitler betrayed the pact, and his troops invaded the Soviet Union, causing great damage to Stalin's military. Stalin refused to back down and defeated Hitler's army, at the cost of around one million Soviet Union soldiers's lives. The loss was a devastating hit to the country, but Stalin continued to fight until the end of World War II. His arrogance and totalitarianism effectively decimated millions of people, including his own, whom he swore to protect. Just like Adolf Hitler, Stalin completely abused his power and caused such significant societal damage that he would go down in history as the man who killed up to 60 million people (Kuroski, 2022).

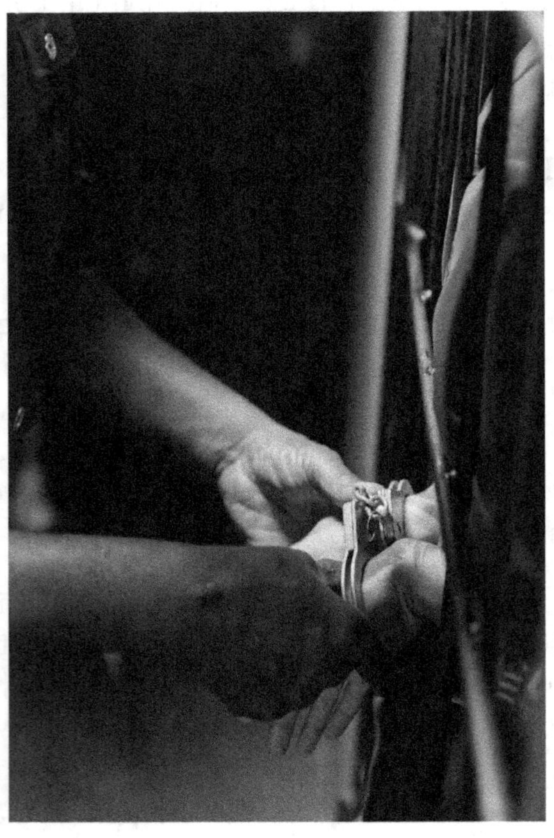

In the early 1970s, a psychologist from Stanford University wanted to conduct his own research about power dynamics among average human beings. In particular, his research focused on the relationships between prison guards and prisoners. The psychologist, Philip Zimbardo, created his own mock prison in the basement of Stanford's psychology building. The simulated prison was designed in the style of American jails. The basement was filled with jail cells and interrogation rooms, in addition to realistic uniforms for both the guards and prisoners.

Zimbardo's experiment involved a group of 24 young men, all of whom were students at Stanford. After signing waivers and contracts, the men were divided into two equal groups. At random, each young man was assigned his role as either a prisoner or prison guard. To ensure the group's commitment to the two-week-long experiment, they were guaranteed compensation upon completion of the study.

The subjects were expected to act according to their assigned roles, without breaking character. Prisoners would spend their days and nights in their cells, being referred to by identification numbers instead of their names. The guards were given the power of acting how they saw fit, as long as they kept their prisoners in order. In the filmed interviews recorded during the two weeks, the men who were assigned roles as prison guards were visibly excited about their assignments. Those that were chosen to be prisoners, on the contrary, were mostly disappointed. The chosen prison guards were given what was seen as the favorable option since they would not have to be subjected to the emotional and physical turmoil that comes with being a prisoner, whether real or simulated.

As the experiment went on, a clear divide was formed between the prisoners and guards. An obvious power imbalance was created. The guards in the experiment took their roles as seriously as they would a real job. They harassed and psychologically abused the prisoners, degrading them so much that they caused true emotional damage. The prisoners, in return, formed an alliance that rivaled the guards. Simply put, the guards were their enemies.

On the second full day of the experiment, the prisoners joined together to rebel against the guards' orders. The prisoners refused to leave their cells for mealtime and wouldn't speak. This angered the guards, who took the rebellion as a personal insult. They took advantage of their power and forced the prisoners out of their clothing, spraying them with fire extinguishers and punishing those who played larger roles in the rebellion. This abuse of power was unrestricted by Zimbardo, who watched the events unfold from a security camera that fed footage to his observation room.

By day six of the simulation, the abuse and brutality became so visibly unethical that Zimbardo discontinued the experiment. The young men portraying the prisoners were battered and bruised, in more ways than one, and the men acting as guards were too consumed with the power of authority.

In the meantime, Zimbardo had reportedly been questioned by his colleagues about the ethicality of the experiment. Apparently, a psychology graduate student objected to Zimbardo's lack of response during the moments of severe abuse. The student, Christina Maslach, argued that the experiment was immoral and had little to no scientific foundation, other than the proof that living in a simulated prison environment would drive people mad (Cherry, 2021). To this day, Zimbardo's experiment is seen as an unethical study that traumatized young college students.

When the experiment is viewed from the perspective of observing power imbalances, it is clear that there were two distinct dynamics at play. Firstly, the false prison guards abused their authority, feeling superior to their peers simply because of the role they were portraying. What's more, the young men took their position of power to the extreme by causing physical and emotional harm to their peers, seemingly without regret or hesitation. The power they were given drove them to act on their violent, aggressive instincts.

The second power dynamic is that of Zimbardo and his subjects. Acting as the prison's warden, Zimbardo watched the ensuing violence as if he were seeing it through a television screen, rather than a security camera. The shocking behaviors of the prison guards rarely caused Zimbardo any concern and he failed to stop the abuse he was witnessing. Some argue that he encouraged the guards to behave as they did, either by not telling them to keep their moral identities in check or by being a passive bystander to the violence. Zimbardo used his own power and authority to indirectly harm his subjects, as well as to give himself the title of the warden, the highest-ranking authority in the simulated prison. Just as it did to the guards, the power went straight to Zimbardo's ego and made him lose sight of his morals and sense of ethics.

The Salem Witch Trials

The Salem Witch Trials, made infamous by Arthur Miller's play *The Crucible*, were a unique example of how religious power can cause societal destruction. In the 17th century, members of a Puritan community in Massachusetts were threatened by the possible existence of witches. Religious leaders at the time believed in the presence of evil in the small town of Salem, existing in the form of female witches. The Puritans believed that these women were capable of summoning the devil, as well as using their powers to commit sins against humanity and, more importantly, against God.

Women living in Salem were subjected to various assumptions, but unmarried women with questionable habits and backgrounds were even more discriminated against. Accusations flew around the town regarding specific women who were believed to be performing witchcraft, which was considered one of the most dangerous sins of all. Salem became a community filled with hysteria about the existence of such sins.

Members of the town were filled with confusion and terror, afraid that a witch would harm them or their faith. Because these people had such a strong belief in the laws of their God, they relied on priests and other religious figures to instruct them on how to deal with the chaotic circumstances. They were told to inform their leaders of any suspicious women, who would then be brought to trial before a judge. If the women were believed to be witches, they would be killed.

The people of Salem were so consumed with their fears that they started falsely accusing women, whether or not they revealed any evidence of witchcraft. Trial after trial, innocent young women were subjected to abuse by the townspeople, some of whom were subsequently murdered. Members of Salem society were filled with a sense of religious power now that they knew they could eliminate practically anyone they wanted, simply by accusing them of being a witch. Though this would typically go against the morals of Puritanism, many people viewed their accusations as a way of fulfilling God's wishes. The trials became commonplace in the town, establishing a reputation of immorality and chaos that remains to this day.

Literary Examples of Power and Corruption

There are countless works of literature that exemplify the dangers of power and how it can corrupt even the most innocent minds. For instance, the Salem Witch Trials may have been a lesser-known piece of history if it weren't for *The Crucible*'s mass popularity. Like Arthur Miller, authors from many parts of the world have recognized the way absolute power destroys societies, drawing inspiration for their own literary works. Novels, short stories, and plays have been written with the intention of establishing an eye-catching and entertaining source for enlightenment. The following examples of such works have been used for decades, even centuries, to teach people about the consequences of letting power go to your head.

1984

George Orwell's classic novel *1984* has been taught to students in the United States for decades. The novel is about a young man named Winston Smith, who lives in a dystopian version of the world following the events of World War II. In this dystopia, the totalitarian government has complete control over its people. The government, called "the Party," enforces constant surveillance and policing of its citizens. No one is allowed to speak negatively about the Party, nor are they permitted to rebel against the totalitarianism to which they are subjected. Anyone who breaks these rules is arrested by the Thought Police, a type of law enforcement that punishes those who disrupt the government's control.

Throughout the novel, the protagonist keeps a journal of his true thoughts about the Party, an act that, if discovered by authorities, would constitute severe punishment. Winston Smith must record his journal entries in secret, hiding from the many security cameras that would report his actions to Big Brother, the eyes and ears of the Party. Over time, he falls in love with a woman and the two have a secret love affair. Unfortunately, Big Brother learns about Winston's resistance to the Party and tortures him, forcing him to face his biggest fear as punishment. Winston eventually succumbs to the torture, losing his will to resist the corrupted government. By the end, the protagonist is converted by the Party and forgets he ever had free will in the first place.

Orwell's novel provides a shocking, albeit over-the-top, example of how corrupt governments are a danger to society. In this case, the Party represents a governmental system that believes it can have total control over its people. The power held by the Party is absolute, leaving little to no room for citizens to act, speak, or even think freely. They are a people completely controlled by their leaders, who in turn are obsessed with maintaining their power.

Lord of the Flies

Similarly to Orwell's *1984*, William Golding's novel *Lord of the Flies* is a common component of American education. *Lord of the Flies* analyzes the concepts of power and corruption through a tale of young castaways.

To summarize, a group of young boys are deserted on an island after a plane crash. Stranded, without any adults or way to communicate with the outside world, the boys look to each other for help. At first, they are able to work together to survive, establishing their own small civilization. They choose a leader, whom they refer to as their chief. However, *civil* is not a word that stays true for the group. With no adult perspective or sense of maturity, the young boys live wildly, making the best of their dire situation as if it were a fun summer camp. They are thrilled to be left to their own devices—no curfews, forced vegetables, or nagging from their parents.

As their time on the island progresses, the group of boys become reckless. The authority of their elected chief, Ralph, is questioned, despite his sense of responsibility and good leadership skills. This leads the group to split into two, one led by Ralph and the other led by the more chaotic Jack. Ralph focuses his group's attention on signaling for help and building shelter, while Jack teaches his group to hunt for food. The groups begin to clash and tensions rise as Ralph and Jack argue with each other's way of leading.

Meanwhile, the groups of young boys are growing fearful of the island. The longer they spend on the island, with no sense of safety, the more they lose their already-limited senses of morality. Witnessing the increasing mayhem, Ralph grows into a more mature version of himself, recognizing the need for civility and democracy. Jack, on the other hand, grows into a savage, violent leader, consumed with power even as a young boy. In the end, three of the boys die; one from the dangers of the island itself, while the other two are killed by their peers.

The novel covers countless themes and concepts, ranging from fear and desperation to the dangers of living without a civilized government. In discussing the issue of power between the two opposing leaders, it has been said that "the desire for power breaks the boys' fragile civilization, causes strife and competition, and ends up destroying the pristine jungle" (Shmoop, 2023). In the end, it is power that destroys any chance of the entire group's survival.

The Lottery

Written by Shirley Jackson, "The Lottery" is a disturbing short story about a community that chooses to play God. Jackson is well-known for her haunting tales that show the more unappealing aspects of human nature. In "The Lottery," the deadly consequences of the power of unfaltering tradition are analyzed.

The story begins with a peaceful description of a small community. The sun is shining, children are playing and filling their pockets with stones—it seems like a wonderful place to live. Members of the community are meandering to the town square, seemingly preparing for an important meeting or announcement. Conversations are being held among the people while the leaders of the town are gathering in front of the crowd. Someone refers to the group assembly as the lottery, a yearly tradition in the town. Once they are prepared, the town leaders call for the group's attention. The lottery is beginning.

The conductor of the event reminds people to grab their stones, which the children have finished collecting and placed in a pile amidst the group. After the group members have each grabbed a stone, the lottery conductor reaches into a black box filled with papers. He retrieves one and reads aloud what is written: a man's name. The man in question is standing among the group with his wife and children, and suddenly the mood of the group becomes tense. The man's wife repeatedly cries that the lottery isn't fair, while the family is told to come up to the black box. The leader of the group presents blank pieces of paper, one for each family member, and draws a black dot on a single piece. The initial contents of the black box are emptied onto the ground in front of the group.

The wife continues crying about the unfairness of the event, but the lottery conductor ignores her and puts the new pieces of paper into the black box, including the one with the black dot. Each member of the chosen family is required to select a piece of paper from the box. Upon selecting, the wife cries harder. She reveals that she has chosen the marked paper.

At the insistence of their leader, the townspeople rush toward the crying woman. They begin to throw their stones at her with vigor, including the members of her own family. She is brutally attacked, crying about how unfair the situation is, bringing the story to a shudder-inducing end (Jackson, 2019).

"The Lottery" is a disturbing commentary on the power of tradition and, consequently, the power gained by those who benefit from the tradition. What began as a pleasant scene full of friendly people transformed into a vicious attack by the same folks, eager to turn against their peer once given the opportunity. Not a single person speaks out against the violent tradition, besides the victim. The townspeople go from happy folk to senseless abusers, all because they are controlled by the power their tradition has over them.

Power Doesn't Have to Be a Bad Thing

As the previous stories have exemplified, power can cause severe consequences when put in the wrong hands. This has been proven consistently throughout history. With the right combination of immorality and false superiority, a person in power can change the world for the worse.

Yet, there are occasions in which power is put to good use. There have been world leaders and social justice warriors who have used their influence to make the world a better place. People like Martin Luther King Jr., Mahatma Gandhi, and Eleanor Roosevelt have made good use of their power by championing human rights and equality, as well as justice for all. The benevolent gods of Egyptian mythology were believed to help humanity survive and prosper, thanks to their divine power and authority. It is only in the hands of those with malintent that power can be a dangerous tool.

As for the god of chaos, power is neither good nor bad. Seth is the perfect example of the subjectivity of morality and the use of power, through his contradicting actions as an Egyptian god. There were times when Seth utilized his power to be a protector and hero for his people and other times when his desire for power caused him to commit the most heinous crimes. He is truly a complex, ambivalent god, one that has never ceased to puzzle researchers and Egyptologists. One message from his mythology is for certain: power can drive anyone mad, even a god.

Conclusion

By now you have been introduced to several concepts unique to Egyptian mythology, as well as ideas about humanity you may have never considered so deeply. Take a moment to allow it all to sink in—the origins of Egyptian gods and goddesses, the incredible influence of their mythology, and the complexities of Seth, the god of chaos. This book has led you through a fascinating and lengthy history, one that will stick with you for a long time. The stories you have learned about are entertaining myths, but they also contain deeper meanings that can impact your understanding of human life.

Seth Means War began with an introduction to the deities of the Great Ennead, the nine gods and goddesses who started it all. You were taught about their special abilities and histories, their distinct imagery throughout history, and their connection to our titular god, Seth. The complex relationships between these gods were described, in detail, to provide you with a better understanding of how the mythological family dynamic truly works.

Along with the intriguing origins of the gods, the first chapter of this book delved into the various concepts that are discussed in every aspect of Egyptian mythology. You have explored the ins and outs of ancient life, from everyday rituals and practices to the ideals that influence every ancient Egyptian person's way of living. The first chapter showed you what it meant to live in honor of the gods and goddesses, following the values defined by the concept of *ma'at*. You now know how important it was to ancient Egyptians to live in truth, joy, and generosity. These values meant everything to the followers of the ancient Egyptian religion. They guaranteed existence in the afterlife alongside the deities they worshiped so wholeheartedly.

You also learned how Egyptian mythology has impacted societies throughout history, including ancient civilizations and modern countries, such as the United States. Chapter 2 went into great detail about the lasting influence of ancient Egypt and its religious beliefs. These beliefs, and the practices that came from them, inspired historic architecture, art, and literature. Wonders of the world were created in honor of Egyptian mythology. Some of the world's greatest artists have depicted famous scenes from the folklore of the gods and goddesses. Even today, in the 21st century, Egyptian mythology has found its place in film and television, as well as in novels and superhero comics. The lasting impact of Egyptian mythology is astounding.

Finally, you were introduced to Seth, the god of chaos. The third chapter of this book brought you to the god's earliest days, explaining his unnatural birth and relationship with his divine siblings. You learned about Seth's complicated family tree, including his rivalry with his brother, Osiris, and his tumultuous relationship with his sister-wife, Nephthys.

In chapter four, you learned why Seth has been depicted so inconsistently in ancient Egyptian art and texts. He took the form of countless creatures and was associated with many others. The fourth chapter discussed how varying perspectives of the god of chaos changed how he was visualized throughout history. For those that honored and worshiped Seth, he was portrayed as a powerful and worthy god. For those who were repulsed by his violent demeanor, the god was shown as a victim or fool. In some places, Seth's imagery was completely eradicated out of contempt for his role in mythology. Here, you were also taught about the many names held by Seth. His name has multiple spellings and pronunciations, and he was known to have several titles and monikers.

Once you learned about Seth's surface identity, you were guided through the complicated stories in which he was portrayed. Chapter five explained how Seth went from a hero god and famous protector to the world's first official murderer, taking his own brother as his victim. Alongside these stories, you were taken on the outrageous adventures of Seth and his nephew, Horus. Their rivalry was unlike any other, resulting in death, decapitation, assault, and, most peculiarly, contaminated lettuce. You were shown how Seth's relationship with Horus not only provided comedic and dramatic content for the ancient Egyptians, but also a background to Seth's purpose as the god of chaos and war.

After reading about Seth's appearances in the famous myths, you were given the opportunity to see how Seth's legacy traveled through time. In ancient Egypt, he was known for his many atrocities and crimes. However, he was not a universally despised god. In the desert lands, where he ruled as the ultimate god, he was worshiped heavily. Temples and tombs were decorated with his iconography and figures were made in his form. Kings even named their sons after the god. Most surprising of all, you learned about the cult that took inspiration from Seth's rebellious nature. Despite thousands of years of new religions and customs, Seth held significant influence, even in 1970s America.

Bringing *Seth Means War* to an end, the dangers of power and corruption were discussed. An intrinsic connection between Seth and humankind was made, revealing that humans may not be so different from the god. You learned of the great consequences that come from absolute power and the desire for absolute power. Like Seth's insatiable need to become ruler of

Egypt, historical and literary figures have proven to lose their morality when power is involved. You saw how the need for control can lead to the destruction of societies, genocide, and worldwide chaos. However, you also learned that human morality is not black and white. It is a concept that cannot be defined, as it is subjective to every person's experiences and beliefs. What may seem morally good to one person could go against the values of another and vice versa.

Morality is a concept that was created by humans for humans, though it will never truly be a concept that is unanimously agreed upon. In the cases of dictators, religious leaders, and even unethical psychologists, morality is completely undefinable. This will be the case for many people, now and forever. Thus, what people do with their power over others will always differ. There will be those who use their power for good, to make positive change in the world, and to fight for those who do not have a voice. Then, on the other end of the spectrum, there will be those who use their power for evil, eliminating free will and causing mayhem.

As Seth has shown us, power can drive a person, or a god, absolutely mad. It can ruin a reputation and destroy families, even those that are divine.

About the Author

As a social scientist, Christopher Fisher has long been fascinated by questions of power and warfare. He has pursued numerous endeavors on the topics, both academically and professionally, with advanced degrees in International Relations, Public Administration, and Ethics & Public Policy. He is also a military veteran with background experience as an intelligence analyst, adding to his incomparable understanding of the human experience. In his free time, the author continues to passionately pursue the stories of our species' colorful past. Since his youth, Mr. Fisher has been enamored by the history of humanity, having fallen in love with ancient Egyptian relics as a young boy. He is an avid fan of ancient Egyptian history and the unique belief systems of the period, particularly those that center around morality and power. In fact, the captivating tales of the Egyptian gods are what originally drove him to study ethics.

Through this book, it is the author's hope and goal to shed light on one of the most infamous deities in all of ancient Egypt: Seth. Though the god goes by many names, he is easily recognized for his affinity for creating chaos in the lives of humans and gods alike. Despite his notoriety, few works of literature delve into Seth's stories from a modern perspective, relating him to the many infamous figures that have existed in more recent human history. Until now.

References

Ancient Egypt Online. (2019). *The Egyptian god Seth.* Ancient Egypt Online. https://www.ancient-egypt-online.com/seth.html

BBC. (2019, November 12). *Joseph Stalin: National hero or cold-blooded murderer?* BBC Teach; BBC. https://www.bbc.co.uk/teach/joseph-stalin-national-hero-or-cold-blooded-murderer/zhv747h

Brazier, Y. (2018, November 16). *Ancient Egyptian medicine: Influences, practice, magic, and religion.* Medical News Today; Healthline Media. https://www.medicalnewstoday.com/articles/323633

Britannica. (2023a). *Ancient Egyptian religion - The gods.* Britannica; Encyclopædia Britannica, Inc. https://www.britannica.com/topic/ancient-Egyptian-religion/The-Gods#ref559415

Britannica. (2023b). *Battle of the pyramids.* Encyclopedia Britannica. https://www.britannica.com/event/Battle-of-the-Pyramids-Egyptian-history

Britannica. (2023c). *Seti I.* Britannica; Encyclopædia Britannica. https://www.britannica.com/biography/Seti-I

Britannica. (2023d). *The satanic bible.* Britannica; Encyclopædia Britannica, Inc. https://www.britannica.com/topic/The-Satanic-Bible

Britannica Kids. (2023). *Nephthys.* Britannica Kids; Encyclopædia Britannica, Inc.

https://kids.britannica.com/students/article/Nephthys/
312673#:~:text=According%20to%20myth%2C%20Neph
thys%20had

Brown University. (2023). *Egyptology and Assyriology.* Department of Egyptology and Assyriology; Brown University. https://e-a.brown.edu/

Cherry, K. (2021, April 16). *The Stanford prison experiment.* Verywell Mind; Dotdash Media, Inc. https://www.verywellmind.com/the-stanford-prison-exp eriment-2794995

Cruz-Uribe, E. (2009). Sth̲ [illegible] pḥty "Seth, God of Power and Might." *Journal of the American Research Center in Egypt,* *45,* 201–226. JSTOR. https://www.jstor.org/stable/25735454?read-now=1#pa ge_scan_tab_contents

Faulkner, R. O. (1937). The Bremner-Rhind papyrus - III. *The Journal of Egyptian Archaeology,* 23(2), 166–185. https://www.reconstructingancientegypt.org/houseofboo ks/wp-content/uploads/2020/03/Bremner-Rhind-Papyr us-III-D-The-Book-of-Overthrowing-Apep.pdf

Fisher, M. (2023, January 16). What 70 years of war can tell us about the Russia-Ukraine conflict. *The New York Times.* https://www.nytimes.com/2023/01/16/world/europe/ru ssia-ukraine-war-attrition.html

Goodreads. (2023). *Egyptian mythology books.* Goodreads; Goodreads, Inc. https://www.goodreads.com/shelf/show/egyptian-myth ology

Goodwin, G. (2021, April). *Changes in the relationship between the Horus and Seth: Set-tling the score.* Phi Alpha Theta Pacific Northwest Conference. https://pdxscholar.library.pdx.edu/cgi/viewcontent.cgi?article=1013&context=pat_pnw

Haikal, F. (2022). *Ra, the creator god of ancient Egypt.* American Research Center in Egypt. https://www.arce.org/resource/ra-creator-god-ancient-egypt

Hornung, E., & Internet Archive. (1982). Conceptions of God in ancient Egypt: The one and the many. In *Internet Archive.* Cornell University Press. https://archive.org/details/conceptionsofgod0000horn/page/136/mode/2up

HubPages. (2015, February 16). *The fight between the Egyptian god Horus and god Seth.* HubPages; The Arena Media Brands, LLC. https://discover.hubpages.com/education/The-Fight-Between-The-Egyptian-God-Horus-And-God-Seth

IMDb. (2023a). *Gods of Egypt.* IMDb; IMDb.com, Inc. https://www.imdb.com/title/tt2404233/?ref_=fn_al_tt_1

IMDb. (2023b). *The Mummy.* IMDb; IMDb.com, Inc. https://www.imdb.com/title/tt0120616/

Jackson, S. (2019). *The Lottery and other stories.* Farrar, Straus and Giroux.

Jerkins, M. (2015, May 19). *Lettuce and kings: The power struggle between Horus and Set.* Michigan Quarterly Review.

https://sites.lsa.umich.edu/mqr/2015/05/lettuce-and-kings-the-power-struggle-between-horus-and-set-2/

Kaufman, S. (2015, September 3). *Does power corrupt everyone equally?* Greater Good Magazine; The Greater Good Science Center. https://greatergood.berkeley.edu/article/item/does_power_corrupt_everyone_equally

Kemet Experience. (2019, March 24). *The 42 ideals of Ma'at.* Kemet Experience. https://www.kemetexperience.com/the-42-ideals-of-maat/

Kiger, P. J. (2021, July 26). *8 facts about ancient Egypt's hieroglyphic writing.* History. https://www.history.com/news/hieroglyphics-facts-ancient-egypt

Kuroski, J. (2022, May 14). *Inside the shocking number of people killed by Stalin during his decades in power.* All That's Interesting. https://allthatsinteresting.com/how-many-people-did-stalin-kill

Lee, J. (2022, March 30). *20 Top-Rated tourist attractions in Egypt.* PlanetWare; PlanetWare, Inc. https://www.planetware.com/tourist-attractions/egypt-egy.htm

Macuno, C. (2021, April 26). *Theocracy: Salem's downfall?* Medium. https://macunocordella.medium.com/theocracy-salems-downfall-38fba6297fa7

Mark, J. J. (2016a, March 28). *Egyptian afterlife: The Field of Reeds.* World History Encyclopedia; World History

Publishing.
https://www.worldhistory.org/article/877/egyptian-after
life---the-field-of-reeds/

Mark, J. J. (2016b, March 6). *Osiris*. World History
Encyclopedia; World History Publishing.
https://www.worldhistory.org/osiris/

Mark, J. J. (2016c, March 7). *Set (Egyptian god)*. World History
Encyclopedia; World History Publishing.
https://www.worldhistory.org/Set_(Egyptian_God)/

Mark, J. J. (2016d, September 21). *Daily life in ancient Egypt*.
World History Encyclopedia; World History Publishing.
https://www.worldhistory.org/article/933/daily-life-in-a
ncient-egypt/

Mark, J. J. (2017a). *Hyksos*. World History Encyclopedia; World
History Publishing.
https://www.worldhistory.org/Hyksos/

Mark, J. J. (2017b, April 11). *Games, sports & recreation in
ancient Egypt*. World History Encyclopedia; World
History Publishing.
https://www.worldhistory.org/article/1036/games-sport
s--recreation-in-ancient-egypt/

Mark, J. J. (2017c, April 25). Apophis. World History
Encyclopedia; World History Publishing.
https://www.worldhistory.org/Apophis/

Mark, J. J. (2019, August 20). *Field of Reeds (Aaru)*. World
History Encyclopedia; World History Publishing.
https://www.worldhistory.org/Field_of_Reeds/

National Geographic. (2017, October 4). *Gods and goddesses of
ancient Egypt*. National Geographic Kids; Creature

Media, Ltd. https://www.natgeokids.com/uk/discover/history/egypt/ancient-egypt-gods/

Niebuhr, R. (2017). *Moral man and immoral society: a study in ethics and politics*. Kessinger Legacy Reprints.

NOVA. (1997). *Pyramids*. NOVA Online; WGBH and PBS. https://www.pbs.org/wgbh/nova/pyramid/explore/age2.html#:~:text=Pyramids%20today%20stand%20as%20a

Orwell, G. (1949). *1984*. Pearson Education.

Rikala, M. (2007). *Once more with feeling: Seth the divine trickster* (pp. 219–240) [Graduate Dissertation]. https://www.academia.edu/63988784/Once_More_with__Feeling

Robinson, J. L., & Topping, D. (2012). The rhetoric of power. *Journal of Management Inquiry, 22*(2), 194–210. Sage Journals. https://doi.org/10.1177/1056492612451789

Rosicrucian Egyptian Museum. (2023). *Explore deities in ancient Egypt*. Rosicrucian Egyptian Museum. https://egyptianmuseum.org/deities-overview

Selden, D. L. (2013). *Hieroglyphic Egyptian: An introduction to the language and literature of Middle Kingdom*. University of California Press. https://books.google.com/books?id=tQVtS54AH9cC&newbks=1&newbks_redir=0&printsec=frontcover#v=onepage&q=demotic&f=false

Shea, C. (2012, October 1). *Why power corrupts*. Smithsonian; Smithsonian Magazine. https://www.smithsonianmag.com/science-nature/why-power-corrupts-37165345/

Smithsonian. (2012). *Egyptian mummies.* Smithsonian Institution. https://www.si.edu/spotlight/ancient-egypt/mummies

Taylor, I. R. (2016). *Deconstructing the iconography of Seth* [PhD Thesis]. https://etheses.bham.ac.uk/id/eprint/7714/1/Taylor17Ph D.pdf

Te Velde, H. (1967). *Seth, god of confusion: A study of his role in Egyptian mythology and religion.* Brill Archive. https://books.google.com/books?id=BR4VAAAAIAAJ&p rintsec=frontcover&source=gbs_ge_summary_r&cad=0 #v=onepage&q&f=false

Tikkanen, A. (2017). Great Sphinx of Giza. In *Encyclopædia Britannica.* https://www.britannica.com/topic/Great-Sphinx

Tour Egypt. (2023). *Egyptian mythology: Great quarrel.* Tour Egypt. http://www.touregypt.net/greatqua.htm

Tousignant, M. (2021, May 5). French leader Napoleon Bonaparte has a complicated legacy. *Washington Post.* https://www.washingtonpost.com/lifestyle/kidspost/wh o-was-napoleon-bonaparte/2021/05/04/a711ee88-a0c9- 11eb-85fc-06664ff4489d_story.html

Turner, P. J. (2012). *Seth: A misrepresented god in the ancient Egyptian pantheon?* [PhD Thesis]. https://pure.manchester.ac.uk/ws/portalfiles/portal/545 24292/FULL_TEXT.PDF

United States Holocaust Memorial Museum. (2019). *German conquests in Europe, 1939-1942.* United States Holocaust Memorial Museum.

https://encyclopedia.ushmm.org/content/en/map/germ
an-conquests-in-europe-1939-1942

Van Zak, G. (1976, November 12). Local Satan worshippers get
set. *Daily Nexus, University of California at Santa
Barbara.*
https://www.alexandria.ucsb.edu/downloads/8s45q9747

Wikipedia. (2022, December 28). *Maat.* Wikipedia; Wikimedia
Foundation, Inc.
https://en.wikipedia.org/wiki/Maat#Afterlife

Wikipedia. (2023, January 1). *Set (deity).* Wikipedia; Wikimedia
Foundation, Inc.
https://en.wikipedia.org/wiki/Set_(deity)#Set_in_the_S
econd_Intermediate

Image References

ArtsyBee. (2016). Egyptian Design Man [Online Image]. In
Pixabay.
https://pixabay.com/illustrations/egyptian-design-man-
woman-priest-1822015/

Azabache, A. (2019). Photo of pyramid during daytime [Online
Image]. In *Pexels.*
https://www.pexels.com/photo/photo-of-pyramid-durin
g-daytime-3185480/

Bonnaire, P. (2021). Ancient Egyptian paintings [Online Image].
In *Pexels.*
https://www.pexels.com/photo/ancient-egyptian-paintin
gs-6448770/

Gomez Pedroso Zamorano, S. (2021). Brown sand under the blue sky [Online Image]. In *Pexels*. https://www.pexels.com/photo/brown-sand-under-the-blue-sky-8272034/

Henriques, M. (2018). Man speaking in front of crowd photo [Online Image]. In *Unsplash*. https://unsplash.com/photos/RfiBK6Y_upQ

Lach, R. (2021). Handcuffs on hands of prisoner in jail [Online Image]. In *Pexels*. https://www.pexels.com/photo/handcuffs-on-hands-of-prisoner-in-jail-10475170/

Mu, M. (2019). Green cabbage vegetable photo [Online Image]. In *Unsplash*. https://unsplash.com/photos/hugb85v0Jo4

Sevim, L. (2022). Egyptian mummy and canup exhibited in museum [Online Image]. In *Pexels*. https://www.pexels.com/photo/egyptian-mummy-and-canup-exhibited-in-museum-11156255/

Shimazaki, S. (2020). Judgment scale and gavel in judge office [Online Image]. In *Pexels*. https://www.pexels.com/photo/judgement-scale-and-gavel-in-judge-office-5669602/

Shumski, R. (2020). Wall carvings in the Karnak Temple in Egypt [Online Image]. In *Pexels*. https://www.pexels.com/photo/wall-carvings-in-the-karnak-temple-in-egypt-6102271/

www.ingramcontent.com/pod-product-compliance
Lightning Source LLC
Chambersburg PA
CBHW071044250726
48653CB00005B/1993